CAT PARTY!

CATS WE'VE KNOWN IN WORDS AND PICTURES

EDITED BY

KATIE HAEGELE

MICROCOSM PUBLISHING

PORTLAND, ORE | CLEVELAND, OHIO

CAT PARTY!: Cats We've Known in Words and Pictures

© Katie Haegele, 2024

First edition – 3,000 copies

ISBN 9781648413100

This is Microcosm # 850

Cover illustration by Matt Gauck
Design by Joe Biel
This edition © Microcosm Publishing, 2024
For a catalog, write or visit:
Microcosm Publishing
2752 N Williams Ave.
Portland, OR 97227

www.Microcosm.Pub/Cats

To join the ranks of high-class stores that feature Microcosm titles, talk to your rep: In the U.S. **COMO** (Atlantic), **ABRAHAM** (Midwest), **BOB BARNETT** (Texas, Oklahoma, Arkansas, Louisiana), **IMPRINT** (Pacific), **TURNAROUND** (UK), **UTP/MANDA** (Canada), **NEWSOUTH** (Australia/New Zealand), **OBSERVATOIRE** (Africa, Middle East, Europe), **Yvonne Chau** (Southeast Asia), **HARPERCOLLINS** (India), **EVEREST/B.K. Agency** (China), **TIM BURLAND** (Japan/Korea), and **FAIRE** and **EMERALD** in the gift trade.

Did you know that you can buy our books directly from us at sliding scale rates? Support a small, independent publisher and pay less than Amazon's price at **www.Microcosm.Pub**.

Global labor conditions are bad, and our roots in industrial Cleveland in the '70s and '80s made us appreciate the need to treat workers right. Therefore, our books are MADE IN THE USA.

Library of Congress Control Number: 2023050203

MICROCOSM·PUBLISHING

Microcosm Publishing is Portland's most diversified publishing house and distributor, with a focus on the colorful, authentic, and empowering. Our books and zines have put your power in your hands since 1996, equipping readers to make positive changes in their lives and in the world around them. Microcosm emphasizes skill-building, showing hidden histories, and fostering creativity through challenging conventional publishing wisdom with books and bookettes about DIY skills, food, bicycling, gender, self-care, and social justice. What was once a distro and record label started by Joe Biel in a drafty bedroom was determined to be *Publishers Weekly*'s fastest-growing publisher of 2022 and #3 in 2023, and is now among the oldest independent publishing houses in Portland, OR, and Cleveland, OH. We are a politically moderate, centrist publisher in a world that has inched to the right for the past 80 years.

CONTENTS

CAT PEOPLE: AN INTRODUCTION

Katie Haegele, illustration by Mocha Ishibashi

*I*n 2017, I wrote a book about cats. I decided it would be called *Cats I've Known,* and I set out to tell stories about every cat I've ever met. To my surprise, I ended up talking about many other things as well—my friends, my childhood, the losses I've lived through, the fun I've had. That's the thing about stories. They're always about so much more than they're about.

Don't get me wrong, though—the book really is about cats. Family pets I had growing up, beloved cats I've shared my home with as an adult, shop cats I take pictures of whenever I visit, strays I bump into on the streets near my house. Each story in the book was illustrated by a talented artist named River Katz, who drew a comic for this anthology, too (p. 43).

A new book, once it's out there, has a way of taking you on a journey; it introduces you to new people, new experiences. With *Cats I've Known,* you won't be surprised to learn, I found myself having *a lot* of conversations about cats. All I had to do was explain the book's incredibly simple premise—"It's just a bunch of stories about, you know, cats I've known"—and people were off and running, telling me stories about their own beloved cats: sweet, sad, ridiculous stories, all of which were idiosyncratic but somehow universal, at least to other cat lovers. This was something of a learning experience for me. I've always loved cats, but having these conversations gave me a new appreciation for cat *people*.

For instance, shortly after the book came out, I went to a booksellers conference in New Jersey to meet people from bookstores and tell them about it. The organizers set me up at a cocktail round loaded with stacks of my books and a marker for signing them. I sat there by myself for a while, picking the label off a bottle of beer and feeling nervous as hell, but it ended up being the sweetest evening. What a conversation starter my book was! One after the other, people took out their phones to show me pictures of their cats and told me stories about the cats' habits that they assumed (correctly) I would find as charming as they did. One woman rolled up her sleeve to show me a tattoo of her cat, done in an old-school portrait style, alongside the others on her arm of rainbows and hearts and her grandmother's face—and later, a guy pushed up *his* sleeve to show me the scars he still had from a roommate's angry cat who'd scratched him years ago. More than a couple of the people I spoke to got tears in their eyes as they talked about a dear cat friend who had died, either recently or a long time ago. I kept nodding sympathetically, tears in my own eyes, tipsy on my one beer. I remember thinking, *I belong here.*

That's where the idea for the *Cat Party* zine series, and now this book, came from. I'd heard too many good cat stories to ignore, so I started collecting them. I asked friends, collaborators, and strangers whose work I admire if they had a story they'd like to share. Maybe in the form of a drawing or a comic, an essay, or a poem? I was very open-minded about the kind of work I would accept, and in the end, I got even more inventive stuff than I was counting on; in this book, you'll find the lyrics to a song ("Frankie, I Miss You," (p. 161), the minutes from a meeting of the Kitty Cat Club (p. 205), and a fantastical comic about a tiny fairy cat the size of a mouse ("Nails," p. 193). Over time, as

I worked with these writers and artists, a kind of community formed. It seemed to me that the creators and readers of the zine constituted a sort of psychic gathering of friends, not bound by place but united by a shared love of cats. You know, like a party.

I put out ten issues of the zine altogether. My partner, Joe Carlough, designed each issue and contributed funny, touching stories and poems to a handful of them, too. Some issues had themes, such as "Lost and Found," for which people reflected on cats who died and ones who ran away—and, in some cases, later came back. The issue I compiled during the endless lockdowns of the pandemic was centered on the idea of home. I've also collected new work specifically for this book: Steven Svymbersky, the founder of Quimby's Books in Chicago and NYC, reflected on the challenges and comforts of having a bookstore cat (p. 38); scholar of medieval literature and lover of spooky stuff, Gina Brandolino, told a story about a cat that might have been haunted by a ghost (p. 18); and legendary punk rock storyteller Joe Genaro memorialized a cat named Bob who liked to drink from the faucet (p. 11). Just as I found with my own book of cat stories, every contribution to this book is like a little window into one of life's bigger themes—loss and grief, safety and belonging, identity in all its many layers.

And before you go off to read those, I have my own story to tell you—the story of an actual cat party I once threw.

For several years, Joe and I shared our home with a round, velvety Siamese mix named Coco. We adopted her from Philadelphia's animal control program, who along with the cat gave us a paper that listed all the information they had about her, including her date of birth and her name, which we kept the same. How they knew her birthday is anybody's guess, but since they did, we knew we were bringing her home just a few days before her thirteenth birthday. An old gal already, but we got to spend six whole years being amused by her large attitude and friendly disposition.

When she turned fifteen, we decided to have a party. Now, Joe and I throw our share of parties, but planning this one was different than usual. We couldn't invite any of our friends who are allergic to cats, of course, and it didn't make sense to invite anyone who would think we were really weird for doing something like this. We also couldn't have folks there who would be so party-hardy that their antics would scare the cat into running upstairs. It was interesting, narrowing the invitation list using these parameters. I'd never thought about my friends in those terms before. We ended up inviting my mother and sister and just four friends, one of whom lives a two-hour drive away, and I truthfully didn't expect any of these people to come. But they all did.

That morning, I gave the house a deep clean, hung up a banner that spelled out M-E-O-W in gold foil balloons, and baked a special "cake" for Coco out of canned tuna and flour using a recipe I found on BuzzFeed. Joe and I put on music to listen to as the guests arrived, and after everyone was there, I switched on Stevie Wonder's "Isn't She Lovely"—Coco's entrance song—and Joe carried her down the stairs and into the party. When I think of this moment, I get tears in my eyes, and I think I'm actually remembering the tears that sprang to my eyes at the time, just over the sweet ridiculousness of it all. It isn't that Joe and I were so dementedly devoted to the cat—well, maybe a little—or that we didn't have anything better to do with our time. It's that we loved each other and the life we made together, me and him and our grumpy, wonderful cat, and making a huge production out of small things has always been our favorite way to show it.

And you know, it wasn't just us. Our friend Helen brought two different party hats for Coco to wear, beautifully decorated paper cones that she had made by hand, complete with ribbons to tie under her chin. Julia took a video of the cat eating her cake and later splashed it up on social media with the caption, "Coco's party was *lit* !" Brandy told us how she had visited a cat-themed gift shop to buy the stuffed carrot toy she gave Coco, then made us laugh by telling us how the lady at the store had looked at her like she was crazy when she asked if they carried birthday cards for cats.

Outgoing creature that she was, Coco sat happily in the middle of all this, munching on her cake and occasionally looking up at the people who'd come to dote on her. I remember how touched I was, not only that our friends had humored us by coming to the party, but that they'd gotten into the spirit of the thing in such a major way. Just as we had, they'd used the party as a way to show us they cared about us, using the coded, creative language employed by sensitive people everywhere.

But of course, that only makes sense, I thought as I looked around at the circle of humans standing in my living room, beaming at Coco and at each other. *They're cat people.*

BOB THE CAT IN THE HOUSE OF BOOKS

Joe Genaro

I took a job once that allowed me to live where I worked. It was something of a dream job. I got to take care of a house of books. My main task was to process orders for what was essentially an online bookstore for used and rare books. The house was literally filled with books, thousands of them. They were in every room except the bathroom and my bedroom. All I needed to do was log into an Amazon account each morning to see which books got sold, look them up in a database, and find them in the house, pick, pack, and ship. I was pretty much left to myself, and it was sweet, at least for the first couple of weeks.

Then, the owner of the business gave me a new responsibility: take care of his aging male cat who had been living in a house that was getting sold. Okay, if he stays out of my room and does not pee on my stuff, I can live with that. My boss put in a standing order for Fancy Feast and cat litter through Amazon, so there'd be no impact on my wallet. Then he showed me a trick. He turned on the faucet in the bathtub so that the water ran in a trickle. The cat, whose name turned out to be Bob, jumped into the tub and started lapping up the water until he had his fill. That's how Bob likes to drink water.

Bob the cat and I got along great at first. He loved sitting on my lap as I watched TV. And he liked to be fed Fancy Feast. I did not mind cleaning his cat litter. And I quickly learned that when Bob would jump into the bathtub it meant he wanted a drink. If I ignored him, he'd get vocal. I also learned that the water had to flow just so. If it was running too fast, he would back away. If it was only dripping, he'd get impatient and give me the eye.

It did not take long for me to realize Bob was a very thirsty cat. I was finding myself attending to the bathtub faucet eight or nine times a day. I had orders to fill, and I couldn't always wait for Bob to finish his drinking, so I started leaving the faucet on, just a trickle, throughout the day. That way Bob could hop in the tub and drink whenever he liked, and I could go about my business packing up the merchandise. That is, until the water bill gave me away. *Don't leave the water running!* I was admonished.

My boss had a solution. He bought, from an Amazon seller, a device made just for cats who prefer to drink running water. It was a motorized "cat fountain" made of plastic. Brilliant! As I assembled it, Bob gave me a terrible stare. It's as if he knew exactly what was going on. In fact, as I later learned, Bob had used one of these things in the past. It's basically a glorified water dish. A pump takes the water from the basin and pours it back into the basin through a spout. The cat is expected to drink the water from the spout. Apparently, there are cats who will not drink still water, and Bob is one of those.

But Bob wanted fresh bathtub faucet water, not almost-fresh fountain water. He refused the fountain. But I was told not to let him drink from the tub. If he's thirsty enough, he'll drink from the cat fountain, the boss told me. He's not going to let himself dehydrate! But I was not so sure.

I stopped turning on the faucet for Bob and he stopped sitting in my lap. It wasn't my imagination. He was upset with me. He walked away when I tried to pet him. I don't handle rejection well. After a couple days, I let him have his faucet water. I made sure I stayed with him so I could turn it off when he finished. And he forgave me.

I decided that Bob was trying to teach me: be patient, stay hydrated. I took it upon myself to have a few sips of water every time Bob jumped in the tub and to spend time with him while he drank.

Remarkably, I started feeling less anxious, more relaxed. I had more energy. I was happier. Bob certainly must have used the cat fountain when I went on vacation, but when I was at the house of books, he got the fresh stuff straight from the source. It was our secret.

Sadly, Bob the cat did not live much longer. He was already a mature fourteen-year-old cat when I met him. He had his last drink from the faucet about a year later. Then he refused his Fancy Feast and passed away, peacefully it seemed, on my lap one morning as I took an extended break from filling book orders.

NA ES AND NICKNA ES FOR A CAT, AND EXPLANATIONS WHEN NECESSARY.

Andrew Keller

allentina: formal name, taken from her very vocal nature, or her howl, a.k.a. the work by allen ginsberg, and tina turner

babygirl: the name on the tag of her collar. also her first nickname.

baby: what we call her now

baby the cat: nice name for a comic book

lil baby: i got really into *my turn* by lil baby in lockdown. especially songs like "can't explain," and "emotionally scarred."

sweet sweet sweet baby girl: (sung to the tune of the "three's company" theme song)

bunny: most cats headbutt for affection and pets; the goodest cat (another nickname) hops like a bunny.

bun

bunny buddy

hopper

sweet bun

my sweet bun

bunita: a portmanteau of "bunny" and "bonita," the spanish word for cute

cloud: she's all white

cloud girl: inspired by "glad girls" by guided by voices. i sing, "hey, cloud girl. only wanna feed you snacks."

cloud belly: from her soft white belly. almost was the name of a food catering business her other human, dana, wants to start.

loaf: baby loves to loaf near the front door.

loafie: like the name sophie

loafer: like the shoe

snuzie: like the name suzie, because she likes to snooze

no-no: (for when she does bad stuff)

lc: long cat

elsie

dumpling: a short-lived nickname. rip dumpling the name, not the cat.

KEVIN AND YUI, SHOT ON 35 MM FILM

Melissa Eismann

TWO CAT STORIES

Gina Brandolino

THE HAUNTING OF TINY

*I*n the early months of 2019, my partner Ellen and I had two cats. Tiny was the rough-and-tumble tabby, a fifteen-pound tough guy of a cat. He was nothing like our other cat Dodds, a dainty, tuxedoed, wide-eyed fella. (*Editor's note*: For a story about Dodds from Ellen's POV, see p. 202.)

That winter, in 2019, Tiny stopped eating all of a sudden—like, all at once. One day he ate breakfast and lunch like usual, then he refused to eat dinner, or anything else. For days. He grew lethargic, wasn't interested in playing; he vomited stomach fluids. Of course, Ellen and I were worried. We took him to the vet, who did some tests and reported the sad news that Tiny was in kidney failure. The vet explained that one of two things was causing it. Option one: sometimes outside cats will get into a toxin, like antifreeze for example, and it settles in their kidneys—if that happens, you can usually flush out the toxin and the cat will be okay. But Tiny wasn't an outside cat, and our house had no toxins in it; we are freakishly careful. So that got us to option two: cats' kidneys are just badly designed and kidney failure is the cause of death of 75 percent of domesticated cats. This seemed to be what Tiny was going through. Our vet said there was no stopping it; we could maybe buy him a little time if we gave him intravenous fluids for three days to help flush out his kidneys, but since his kidneys were failing, inevitably, he would slip back into poor health again—maybe in a few weeks, maybe in a few months. So we did the fluids, and Tiny did feel better, slowly at first, but steadily. And he stayed better.

After well more than a few months passed, Ellen and I were reflecting on Tiny's miraculous recovery, trying to figure out how to explain it. Maybe he did get into something toxic? But we are so cautious, and to be honest, if any cat in our house was going to eat something and get sick, it's going to be the simpler, less savvy, more food-motivated Dodds. So how to explain this? What had happened right before Tiny became ill? Then we both remembered at the same time, with a sick feeling: the ghost hunter had visited our house.

My ghost hunter friend Tim uses modified radios, also known as ghost boxes, to contact spirits. We had asked him to come over and see what he could hear at our house, and we had a pretty good session: some folks from the other side talked to us, seemed to really try to establish a connection, then eventually faded out. But something strange happened while Tim was there, stranger than the voices from the other side on the radio: Tiny came out and sat with us. Tiny was not a social cat; he loved, I mean truly adored, Dodds and grew comfortable with asking Ellen and me for affection, but he wasn't ever really into other people and usually didn't come around when people he didn't know well were over. So when he came for the ghost box session, we thought Tiny just liked Tim. After the session was over, we went to give Tiny and Dodds dinner and that was the first time Tiny refused to eat. Had the contact with the other side caused it? But how?

I was able to make sense of what happened to Tiny only by having learned a lot from Tim. He's a kind, steady, knowledgeable guy who believes there's no such thing as an evil spirit, just a crabby or jerky spirit, and he's dealt with his share of them. He told me a story once of having an "attachment"—a spirit who sort of gloms onto you and is hard to shake. Tim's experience was that he felt sick, just really really sick, for a while—until the attachment detached. Drinking water helped. Ellen and I decided Tiny probably had an attachment—not a digestible toxin, but a spiritual one, one that he eventually shook off, or it left of its own accord. And maybe all the water—the IV fluids—helped. Tim agreed—this sounded right to him—and he issued a warning on his social media that people interested in paranormal study should remember the effects it might have on pets.

A week or so after we realized this, by pure chance, we got a free smudging kit in the mail with something else we had ordered, and we smudged the hell out of Tiny. He thrived for a while, but eventually kidney failure did take him. I don't think the ghost box speeded his demise; I feel more like it alerted us to a problem we then knew to watch. And I'm sure Tiny pays ghostly visits to his tuxedoed brother Dodds.

NAMING A CAT

When I was twenty-five years old, I moved from the city in the south Chicago suburbs where I grew up to Bloomington, Indiana to start a doctoral program. It was the first time I lived on my own, and I loved my apartment, but it had mice. The solution was never going to be mousetraps or poison—I wanted something that would keep the mice from ever coming in. That, I imagined, was a cat: mice would get a whiff of a cat and move on to the next apartment, I figured.

I could have gone to the local humane society to get a cat, but my mom suggested I take one from the sort of ramshackle compound my stepdad's family lived on. His sister had cats but wasn't good about neutering or spaying them, so there were literally dozens living in a series of barns and outbuildings. One of the cats, who the kids living on the property called Wolf, distinguished himself by constantly sneaking into my stepdad's parents' house and sleeping in the laundry. "This cat wants to be an inside cat," they said, so they got him neutered and had him driven down to me.

I knew right away he was no Wolf. For one thing, he didn't resemble any wolf I'd ever seen—he was long-haired and totally white except for a black cap, a black tail, and a few stray black spots on his paws. He came to me looking full-grown, but he kept growing and eventually was three feet tip-to-tip, nose to end of tail. He also didn't act like a wolf: He wasn't frightened or angry about being inside. He was sociable and friendly and polite; the first thing he did was use the litter box, like he'd been an inside cat all his life. Then he jumped up and primly sat on the couch, a total gentleman. I half expected him to ask if I had any magazines he could peruse. So: it was clear he needed a new name.

He got it in a moment of destiny. I was standing in my apartment looking down at him, and I said, "What am I gonna call you, sweet pea?" I don't know where that came from; "sweet pea" isn't a term of endearment I have ever used often. It just came out, and it stuck.

It's an unusual name, and it sometimes caused confusion. Upon meeting Sweet Pea, a lot of people would assume he was female. "No," I'd correct them, "like Popeye's son!" And then they'd get it. Once a receptionist at a veterinary office mistyped his name as "Sweat Pear." His closest friends called him Pea. He was very photogenic, a true beauty, and often photographed; I have many pictures of him, and they're always turning up as memories on social media. And though he's been gone a decade, if I post a picture of him on social media, all those old friends show up to remember him.

In case you're curious, I was right about the mice; I never had any more of them. Once a vole got in, but Pea stood sentinel watching it until my friend Kyle came over and got it safely back outside. This wasn't anywhere near the best part of living with him, though. It's hard to say what was because he was such an amazing companion.

We figure Sweet Pea was a year old when I got him and seventeen or eighteen when he died. He was with me a long time, and through so much: through my whole doctoral program, from my very first classes through my dissertation writing to my PhD; through coming out to my parents; through four apartments and two houses. He charmed all of my girlfriends but absolutely bonded with the one who has become my beloved partner. He's the cat in whose honor I take care of all others I'll ever have; even though I love them all for all their own special qualities, there just won't ever be another Sweet Pea. He will always occupy the comfiest place in my heart.

HI I'M MOMO AND I LIVE HERE NOW

Heidi Moreno

HI I'M MOMO & I LIVE HERE NOW

BY: HEIDI MORENO

SUPER CHILL *CHILLIN*

JANVARY

MOMO'S FIRST VISIT

I SHOW UP WHENEVER I WANT. I HAVE A VERY CHILL SCHEDULE.

I LIKE TO LAY LOW SO NO ONE SEES ME.

≈ COMMANDO CRAWL ≈

THAT'S MY EARTIP. I GOT IT IN MAY. I DUNNO WHY, BUT I FEEL FASHUN NOW. ANYWAYS, MY MOM (LADY WITH THE GOOD FOOD & WATER) SAID MY LIFE IS ABOUT TO GET BETTER. I'M EXCITED

I USED TO ROAM
AROUND ALL NIGHT.
SOME DAYS WERE
REALLY SCARY. BUT
NOW, I SLEEP ALL
DAY IN MY MOM'S
BACKYARD.

JULY

MEEEOOW

IN AUGUST I STARTED TO
CRY A LOT WHEN MY
MOM + DAD WOULD GO BACK
INSIDE THEIR HOUSE. I
WANTED SCRITCHES ALL DAY.

ONE NIGHT MY MOM CAME HOME
LATE AFTER WATCHING A LIVE BAND.
I MEOWED AT HER & SHE PICKED ME
UP AND TOOK ME INSIDE. I SAID THANK
MEW BY CUDDLING ALL NIGHT.

AND THAT'S PRETTY
MUCH HOW THE
COOKIE CRUMBLED.
I HAVEN'T SLEPT
OUTSIDE SINCE THAT
NIGHT. TWO WEEKS LATER I MOVED INSIDE.
I HAVE A SISTER NOW TOO. HER NAME IS
PEANUT. SHE'S FEISTY BUT I LIKE HER. SO
YEAH... I LIVE THERE NOW. *THE END*

CURIOUS GENDER

Key K. Bird

When we first met, my snowshoe companion, Ezra, had a different name. The adoption center had named her Alfreda. It didn't suit her. It was too stiff, too formal, too feminine. Ezra proved it wrong the first chance she got. As soon as she was out of her cage, she ran to the fence that separated her from another nearby cat. She stalked other animals. Her stare was stark. I tried to get her attention—but Ezra hissed at me, then lost interest in both me and the other cat entirely, instead turning her snout to gauge her newfound freedom. She hopped up beside my best friend, crawled onto the back of his chair, and put her front feet on his shoulder to claim him. That was how she became family. She walked up and demanded it.

We named her Ezra, a so-called 'boy's name' that I chose for its palindromic form: vowel, consonant, consonant, vowel. A mirror. And she lived up to the name, reflecting me again and again.

But Ezra was so much more than her name, so much more than my tendency to see myself in her. She was stubborn. She once ate through a wax bag to wolf down half a scone. She was gentle. She fretted over us and slept by our sides whenever we felt sick. She was goofy. Her face when she woke from a hard nap was a tender, frenzied shock.

Ezra's gender, if anything at all, was curious.

During our time together, we saddled Ezra with a dozen nicknames. The first one was Fez—sometimes, the Fez. Whenever she hid, we'd ask each other, "Have you seen the Fez?" It rhymed with the first syllable of her name, so it made sense as a shortened version of Ezra, but when I give friends nicknames, they also include their given names. Which is how my friends Gillian, Tedd, and

Randolph became Gillibean, Teddley, and Rampersandolph. So it went that Ezra became Ezra-Fez or, when we sang it, Ezra-Fezra.

But I wish I could've asked Ezra what she called herself. What sound, which utterance, what inner thrum did she use to think of herself? I answered to another name for nearly forty years, but never used it internally. Before renaming myself, I only ever called myself *you*. But since my new name, I treat myself more like a friend. I think up different iterations of my name. Key B., KB., Key K., Mys. Bird. (Mys. is short for Mystery, and phonetically contains both Miss and Mister.)

I always felt strange hearing people say my given name. It didn't fit. Like Alfreda, it was formal, stiff, feminine. And like Ezra, nobody had ever asked me what I called myself.

Admittedly, we almost didn't keep Ezra. Within the first two weeks that we lived together, my face was blotchy and it wouldn't calm down. I don't know that it was her. It didn't make sense. I'd had three cats before. I'd never been allergic. My best friend was allergic. We'd adopted her anyway. But he was in better shape than I was. I was unspeakably sad.

We made the hard decision to take her back. I went so far as to call and schedule the appointment to drop her off. And the instant I hung up the phone, she looked at my face, and, I swear, she knew. She looked so small and confused and afraid. It was the first time I saw myself reflected in her. Abandonment issues writ large. I called the shelter again and apologized: "I can't do it."

I've given up on myself countless times throughout my life. I've mistreated myself, put myself last, grown impatient with myself, gotten fed up with my chronic illness, given myself every reason to put off my needs and desires because that was easier than figuring out how to value myself the way I would a friend. Keeping Ezra, who I very much wanted in my life, and figuring out my health problems was one of many times she helped me grow. Loving Ezra taught me how to accept the parts of myself I'd learned to resent.

Living with two writers, Ezra endured the brunt of our inventions about her life. We narrated everything she did. We recited dialogue back and forth in a voice we pretended was hers. In that way, she spoke to us, reprimanded us, asked us questions, told us what strange cats we were. But she never said our names. To her, we were Tall and Taller. On the rare occasion that she referred to herself, we called her Small.

This bit of stage business allowed us to pull Ezra into the future with us. We always included her in conversations about our hopes and dreams and fears. So, when we thought about scary things, upsetting truths like death, our own mortality, and even the end of the world, of course, we thought of how Ezra would fit into the picture. A year or so after our seventh wedding anniversary, a year after we adopted Fez, I turned to my best friend, and not wanting to upset him, launched into an absurd premise: "So, let's say I got some sort of once-in-a-lifetime offer to travel to deep space, where I would explore . . . something literary, and—I don't know—otherworldly, I guess. Of course, I'd have to say yes, right?" This was years before super-rich people were traveling to the moon for evil deeds. "The thing is, by the time I got back, space travel being what it is, everyone we know would be gone. Because quantum physics. So, my point is, if that happened, I'd want you to be happy. Really, truly, happy with someone else."

To his credit, my best friend didn't get upset over this announcement. He saw I was trying my best to come up with something funny to lighten my fear. But, of course, I wasn't done. "The thing is, that person is *not* allowed to be Tall. No matter what. There is only one Tall." And not only that: "Instead, Ezra will call that person Barbara."

And we laughed and laughed because, wasn't I clever? Wrapping this sad thing in a funny thing to make it less horrific. Me, deep space, cheating death. Ha ha ha ha ha.

But, again, that wasn't all. Within days of this conversation, we decided that since I was Tall, and my best friend was Taller, then anyone—anyone—who wasn't Tall or Taller had the potential to become Barbara. And so, to Ezra, everyone who wasn't me or my partner became Barbara. Regardless of gender. Amazingly, all of our friends went along with it. We'd hang out with them, and they'd say, "Tell Ezra Barbara said hello." They'd send her text messages, entire emails for Ezra, signed "Love, Barbara."

I'd remember this years later, seven years after the original Barbara conversation, when I started telling my closest friends I had changed my name. To my surprise, some of them said, "I've always wanted to change my name." And they had names already chosen. No wonder they had been so ready to become Barbaras. There had always been other versions of themselves they'd hoped to be.

In Arabic, Ezra means help. I learned that after I'd broken my leg in two places and was bedridden for eight weeks, but once I'd given it thought, it made complete sense. She helped me in ways I couldn't help myself.

When I was in the hospital, I couldn't do much at all. I couldn't get up to use the bathroom. So I couldn't wash my face or brush my teeth. I used a catheter for days. There's a photo of me, taken a few days after my surgery. I look mean. It reminds me of the first photo I saw of Ezra. She was also recovering from surgery—she'd been pregnant when they found her; they aborted the kittens—and, in the photo, Ezra also looked mean. Stuck in a borrowed bed, not allowed to leave, stitched up after something scary. The staff members at the adoption center had been surprised we wanted to take her home. I resented their surprise. But when I was waiting for clearance to go home, I'm not sure I would've wanted my own company.

I had to slide up two flights of stairs backwards to reach my apartment. My leg was in plaster. I didn't know how to use crutches on stairs yet. I was in so much pain, physical and emotional, by the time I got in. But Ezra ran to see me, curious as ever, but also aware—I was hurt. I needed her. She came to my rescue.

A metal rod had been threaded into my tibia, anchored with screws at my knee and my ankle. Because I couldn't put weight on my leg for the first few weeks after the surgery, a nurse visited our apartment to make sure there were no complications. She's the one who told me about the meaning of Ezra's name and also that her presence might literally hasten my recovery.

Ezra was indeed ready to help. Every time I was in bed, she stepped all over my cast, walking in circles to find the best angle before plopping down on my leg and purring so hard it rocked her back and forth. Her purr sounded like heavy rain, and frequently throughout my bedrest, that sound lulled me to sleep.

Cats purr for all sorts of reasons: communication that says "I'm happy," residual habits from kittenhood when they purred to be fed, and an attempt to calm down after something upsetting. The sound of purring literally heals wounds. There are several studies about the sound frequency of purring: 25–100 Hertz. That frequency is therapeutic in healing broken bones in cats and humans alike. Ezra lent me that particular brand of self-repair. She knew, strange cat that I was, that I couldn't heal myself on my own.

When I went in for an X-ray three and a half months after the break, the doctor said it usually takes nine months before they can determine whether a break has healed. But based on that X-ray, my fracture was almost invisible. She couldn't technically call it a union, but the doctor said it was remarkably close. While I can't credit Ezra entirely—I had the privilege to work from home during the first few weeks after surgery, and my best friend drove me to and from work every week after that—Ezra stayed by my side every time I was laid up in bed. She taught me to care both for and about myself. She taught me to be my own friend.

My best friend and I often joked that Ezra had inherited parts of us. She had a dark squiggle down the middle of her face, so her nose was asymmetrical like mine. She was fretful and prone to indigestion like my best friend. She had mysterious allergies like I do. Like me, she was multiracial with ancestral ties to Asia. She was so pretty that people always said so, much like they do when describing my best friend.

There were certain things she did that we couldn't connect to ourselves. She hated shadows. They frightened her. She would cry and run in circles if the shadows in one room traveled to the next. When we moved apartments (which she did with us three times), she ran around the new place every time like she'd won the kitty lottery. I could only guess the cause of that behavior: "I think she was afraid we were going to leave her behind."

My mirror. My abandonment issues. She deserved a better inheritance.

Then again, so did I. My chronic illness might be genetic. It manifests in forty-some regular symptoms, many of which are dermal issues. Itching, flaking, scabbing skin. In the last half of her life, Ezra groomed parts of her legs bare. And once she'd licked off the fur, she went at them until she had sores. I now suspect it was because she was sick and didn't know how to tell us—Ezra died at eight and a half years old from cancer, which I've since learned happens to many snowshoe cats. But at the time, all we could do was worry. We didn't know how to help her. She was misdiagnosed over and over. Stress, allergies, gum infections, kidney disease, "old" age. As someone with chronic illnesses and a decade of misdiagnoses, including some that amounted to psychosomatic ailments, I sympathize and rage on Ezra's behalf. The last doctor she saw, before a different doctor found tumors in her intestine, told me that tests would be expensive. He didn't tell me what the tests might have revealed, only that they'd be costly. Translation: not worth the expense.

That doctor didn't give me enough information to let me decide that for Ezra or myself. By the time I spent the money, and I spent it without hesitation, it was far too late to help Fez. All we could do was give her medicine that made her hurt less. I think of the number of human women and gender nonconforming people whose pain gets ignored and overlooked by doctors. In that sense, and so many others, I wish Ezra had inherited something far better than we did.

I was beside myself with grief before the end. I wanted whatever solace I could get. So I looked through all the photos I had of Ezra and found one where she wore a little black bowtie attached to a white shirt collar. I wrote what I could bring myself to say about Ezra's illness and posted it alongside the photo on social media. A friend left a comment on the androgynous portrait: "Like mother, like daughter."

I couldn't hold back the sobs. I wasn't her mother. She wasn't my daughter. I was her Tall. She was my Small. She was my Ezra. My Fez. My Smidge. My Sprocket. My Squiggle. My Monkey. My Beansprout. My little Rorschach Face. My raccoon panda. My loudymouth. My friend. Her names. There were so many. I wish I'd known her real name. I wish I could ask her. I wish I could tell her my new name. I'd respond in her voice, which was always deadpan and always loving nonetheless: *That's great, Tall. Now you're you.* I never said kinder words to myself than when I spoke to me as her. I wish I could tell her how she helped me. I wish I could tell her what it meant to have her look at me and not care what I wore or whether my given name chafed or whether I felt like myself. I wish I could tell her how I loved her life and how much of it she spent with me. I wish I could tell her that being with her every day changed my life, and how it always hurt to leave her. Every single time, the whole time we knew her, not just at the end.

After adopting Ezra, whenever we left on a trip, we'd be gone for maybe fifteen minutes before one of us would say, "I miss the Fez." And on our way back, we'd always play the same guessing game.

One of us would start off with something like: "I'm thinking of something . . . little."

"Okay. Hmm. Something little. Is it—lima beans?"

"No. Not lima beans. I'm thinking of something . . . fuzzy."

"Little and fuzzy, huh? Let's see. Is it—pocket lint?"

"Nope. Not pocket lint. I'm thinking of something little and fuzzy that also has a great big loudymouth."

"Oh, I think I know! Is it . . . Ezra?"

"It is Ezra!"

Then we'd switch roles and come up with three new hints, round after round.

And when we got home, Ezra would drop to the floor, rolling back and forth on her back, showing us her tummy, and purring, always purring, while squeezing the air between us. That reach of hers said *yes* and *finally* and *more* and *what took you so long?* It was the worst example of ladylike behavior. I couldn't have had a better guide. In terms of healing, in every sense, I couldn't have had better help.

CAT AND PIE GO ON A WALK

Defectivepudding

Cat & Pie go on a walk !!!!

BY DEFECTIVEPUDDING

One day a pie was made.

but before a piece could cool...

it sprouted arms, legs, and a face and ran away!

The pie thought it had escaped death, well at least for that day.

There also was a witch's apprentice, who was extremely lazy!! Who happened to be asleep when all of a suddon...

a piece of pie ran by!

sniff sniff

the cat stood up and said...

before the pie could pass by

Hello my lil pie

The pie waited...
...without...
...suspicion.

and with
a snap and
gulp,
the lil pie met
the cat's other
friends.

THE END

QUIMBY'S CATS

Steven Svymbersky

*I*t always surprises me when I meet bookstore people who are not also cat people. I assume bibliophiles are inherently ailurophiles, just like I assume fans of *Cat Party* know what both those terms mean.

Bookstore cats are a profound example of our civilization, combining our desire for knowledge and animal companionship. I'm of a mind that all bookstores should have at least one cat. I don't think they all need to be full of kittens you can adopt, like at Otis & Clementine's Books in Nova Scotia—but I wouldn't object to that either.

When I opened a bookstore in the '90s (Quimby's in Chicago), I already had a cat, Lizzie Borden, a petite, tortoiseshell calico with a sour disposition. She adored me and I her, but she had lived with me in small apartments for over a decade and adapted to living in a large bookstore by making it clear she wasn't interested in strangers. She also had to put up with a very sweet but dumb German shepherd named Magoo. Poor Magoo didn't stand a chance against Lizzie, and I was forever pulling claws out of his snout.

The reason Lizzie lived in the store was that my new partner/roommate also had a cat, Persephone, a gorgeous, white, long-haired princess. Lizzie had earned her reputation as a demon by leaving every cat she ever lived with over the years (a few!) with at least one bifurcated ear. It was clear Persephone would be no match when it came down to territory, so she stayed home while Lizzie, at the age of eleven, became a bookstore cat. I believe she mellowed a bit over the years thanks to the more social environment.

When I opened a second Quimby's in Brooklyn in 2016, I did not get a cat right away. I don't think it even occurred to me at first. There were so many other things I had to do to create a space and keep it open. The odds of a small store selling zines succeeding in NYC were not great. It was wise to be sure

I had some stability before adding live animals into the mix. Additionally, there was also an issue with the front and back doors, which I propped open when it was warm. Behind the store is a parking lot, and in front is a very busy street. I can screen the back door, but the front door is metal with no way to add a screen door. I could imagine a cat running out into traffic, and I didn't want that on my conscience.

Like a lot of people, though, during the pandemic, I yearned for feline companionship. I knew that once I put the word out that I wanted a cat, one would come to me. It wasn't long before I heard about three young stray cats that had wandered into the backyard of a couple in Bushwick. This couple already had plenty of cats in their apartment so they couldn't take them in, but they built a shelter by their garage, fed them, and started trying to find homes for them. When I contacted them, they warned me that the kittens, which were about nine months old at that point, had never been indoors and would not let anyone near them. They were feral, and it would take some time to domesticate.

I could only take one, but I did not blink or think for a second that this would be a problem. Cats love me. I pride myself on being able to woo even the starchiest of cats. People would tell me, "Gosh, that cat doesn't like anybody," as it sat contentedly purring in my lap. I got the good cat gene. Cats can tell. And I am a master petter. It's an art.

So in the beginning, I brought Fishpaw, a skinny, gray tiger, into the store with great optimism. He immediately ran and hid. And he continued to hide. There were many days when I nearly went crazy trying to find where he was hiding, wondering if he was hiding or if he had somehow escaped. Apparently, he would come out at night, when I wasn't there, to eat and use the litter box, but during the day he would hide. If I found him, he shook in terror at the sight of me.

There was one stretch of a few days when I could not find him anywhere, but every morning his food bowl was empty. Eventually, I figured out that he had climbed the indoor, roll-down security gate and found a hole in the ceiling. He was between the walls! I had to trick him by pulling the gate down at night and waiting outside for hours until he finally climbed down the gate and went to the back of the store to eat. On my first attempt I was not fast enough, and by the time I had the gate halfway up, he had dashed from the back of the store, jumped on the counter and then the gate, and disappeared into the ceiling again before I could even yell, "Stop!"

After many months, I thought maybe I was getting somewhere. I would sit reading, unmoving on the couch, and Fishpaw would come out from under the couch and stare at me. After a while, he didn't run away immediately if I started cooing to him. But I was never able to make a move that wouldn't send him back to his sanctuary. After six months, Fishpaw had not overcome his abject fear at being trapped, caged inside this strange place. It broke my heart a bit that my special cat powers had failed me.

After nearly eight months, he did finally escape. I had the whole neighborhood looking for him. Every night I set a bowl of food out back in the parking lot and sat twenty feet away watching for him. He never came back.

It wasn't just that my powers had failed me; I had failed Fishpaw. And that failure, coupled with the thought of Fishpaw—or any cat—roughing it on the streets of Brooklyn, made me decide that having a cat in this store just wasn't a good idea. I had learned my lesson.

Fortunately, the story doesn't end there.

At Christmas dinner in 2022, a couple of months after Fishpaw had escaped, my friend Larra, a certified cat lady, insisted that she had the perfect cat for me and the bookstore. I protested and told her the tragic story of Fishpaw, but she refused to take no for an answer. I agreed to at least meet this cat.

Larra had named the cat Scanner because her eyes go back and forth when she is focusing on something. Scanner had first wandered into Larra's yard looking as if she hadn't been on the street long: she was clean and well fed, and her front paws had been declawed. Despite Larra's best efforts to find the owners, no one claimed her. As a certified cat lady, Larra has a house full of cats and is constantly fostering new ones, but her cats didn't like Scanner, so Larra and her partner had to keep her in the basement. Scanner needed a home.

I didn't keep the name Scanner, but I fell in love with the cat, who is now called Gracie because she's so graceful.

Let me tell you about her. She's a big girl. Ten pounds or more. She's mostly white but with a big, brown, cat-shaped patch on her back and black and brown ears and tail. Her fur is soft like a rabbit's. She has stunning blue eyes. Maybe she's around six years old? As soon as she appeared in the store she warmed it with her sweetness and beauty. She rubbed her nose on my face the first moment I met her.

Gracie is a quintessential bookstore cat. She sleeps for much of the afternoon in a cardboard box on the counter where I wait on customers. I have tried giving her several different cloth and pillow beds but no, she loves her box. She looked so cramped, curled up in it, that I also tried giving her a bigger box. I tried putting a cushion in the bottom, too. She spurned both improvements.

She is not shy about rubbing herself around customers' ankles. Of course, the customers love her, and she has many regular visitors. She is, frankly, very good for business. She makes no attempt to run outside, seemingly unwilling to take the chance of being trapped on the wrong side of the door, but she loves to sit in front of it and watch the world go by—especially when pigeons feed on the sidewalk. She does this strange thing where she rubs her paw up and down the glass door. It reminds me of Maneki-neko, the Japanese good luck cat that waves. Many people stop and take photos of her. Sometimes they come into the store.

She jumps out of the way when customers enter the store, but she makes them step over her when they exit.

Don't you love that? Having to step over a cat as you exit a shop?

My only issue with having a cat in the store—one that sleeps on the counter—is that there are some busy days when she is constantly being woken by overeager petters. I know she wouldn't stay there if she hated it, but I can also tell she kinda hates it. And she bites, not hard, but she has very sharp teeth. So, be considerate of shop cats, whether they're in a bookstore, bodega, or otherwise. Check in with the proprietor first. Maybe they'd prefer you let the cat sleep.

I had Lizzie Borden, the original Chicago Quimby's cat, for twenty years. I still have her ashes. I can only hope Fishpaw is happy living the life of an outlaw somewhere in Brooklyn. I know I feel more civilized with a cat by my side, and I know my bookstore is more magical for Gracie's presence. I'm grateful for her every day.

HOME IS WHERE MY CATS ARE

River Katz

ANCHORS

Rebecca Bayuk

*T*hree days after Christmas, Patrick arrives.

My friend has texted me while we were away back East. Her father is ill, and she has flown home to be with him; her friend has Patrick right now, but won't be available much longer. Can we take him for a few days?

I've met Patrick once already, at my friend's birthday party a few months before. He was wearing a bow tie, and I had my picture taken with him early in the evening, when he was hanging out watching TV upstairs, away from the noise, relaxing before he went to sleep. I sent my sister the picture, my face shiny and smiling and pressed up to his, the image with its emoji-laden caption winging its way across the Atlantic and into her inbox as her day began and ours ended.

My friend is concerned about asking me to take him, because it's not planned, is coming out of nowhere, and because I've spent the last week in bed, missing all the festivities at my boyfriend Tom's family home because I've had the flu, the worst I've had in years.

I'd lain in bed upstairs all week, sweating and aching, crying in the middle of the night that my skin hurt, my limbs hurt, and why wasn't the medicine working? Minutes had pooled into hours into days, and I'd lain there, first in one room and then another, as family members flew back to their homes and long, drawn-out farewells were conducted in the hallway below me. I missed most of these goodbyes, ebbing in and out as I was of a thick, clammy half-sleep, punctuated by Tom bringing me more water, more medicine; punctuated by strange fever-dreams in which I heard phrases and sounds repeat over and over, spooling out again and again like oily wool.

I'm starting to feel less awful, can move around now, managed at least the flight home, all drug-muffled from the pills I'm taking with military precision every four hours. Tom is now getting sick, too. I'm feeling guilty. Guilty for giving it to him, and guilty for missing everything during our visit.

But Tom is not feeling quite as bad as all that, he says, and will be going back to work in a couple of days. So Patrick is welcome, I tell my friend. I'll just be lying around anyway, shaking off the last of it, so I might as well have company.

It won't count as getting a cat of our own, this visit of his, after all.

Patrick arrives that evening, ushered carefully across the threshold of our second-floor condo by the girl who's been caring for him. She asks us to excuse her a moment, and dashes back down the steps to her car so she can retrieve his things, bring them back up and set them down carefully next to where he waits patiently. A couple of heavy bags, a litter tray, a scoop we'll find months later behind the dryer and forget to return.

After she leaves, we shut and lock the door behind her. We glance at each other over Patrick's head, unsure of ourselves for a second, of our abilities to care for him, now that he's actually here in our living room.

Some unspoken agreement must pass between us, because we break the silence and welcome Patrick enthusiastically in gentle, singsong voices, crouch down so our faces are more level with his as he emerges from the carrier. He looks fairly unimpressed with our efforts, but not entirely hostile, so I take this as a good sign, and we encourage him to start exploring the place, to take a look around, to make himself at home.

Even though I've done this before, been here before, albeit on a different continent, during a different time in my life, I'm nervous, and slightly giddy with it, skittish despite feeling washed-out and limp after a week in bed. I stand awkwardly by the table in the dining area. Tom quietly follows Patrick about at a respectful distance, watching what he does, where he goes, reluctant to sit back down.

Eventually, though, we do sit. We don't want him to feel pressured or stressed, we agree: the change of scenery is likely making him anxious enough, poor thing. I feel a twinge of guilt at this. I wonder if cats can understand this tendency of ours to move them about, to open up, again and again, the doors of their carriers to rooms they don't recognize. I wonder if they worry for their owners and where they have gone. Do they look up at us, these strangers with gormless smiles, and recognize allies, or are they simply desperate for the familiarity of their owner's face, for their smell?

After several minutes in which we try—unsuccessfully—to watch TV, we hear a soft little thump and turn to see Patrick standing squarely on the counter in the kitchen, fixing us with what I am sure is an amused expression.

We watch as he leaps gracefully to the top of the fridge and from there to the top of the cupboards which line the wall of the kitchen; there's not much space between them and the ceiling, but it's big enough for Patrick to crouch in, as it turns out.

They like to do that, Tom says, watching him. I'm sure I've heard before that they like to do that, to get up high and watch everything. Like lookouts.

I agree with him, nodding. I remember how they like to climb, to perch—to gaze, unruffled, over their kingdoms. I imagine another cat sitting atop a painting ladder, observing a different kitchen, swathed in dust-sheets.

Yes, they do like to do that, I say. Funny, isn't it, how they like to do that.

Patrick fixes us again with his green-gold eyes. He jumps down onto the tile, and step by deliberate, delicate step, he makes his way over to the sofa, the back of which we are both leaning over breathlessly to see what he will do next. Playing it cool, we are most decidedly not.

Every few steps, Patrick brings his face, sleek and narrow, to the air and sniffs at it gently. He brings his face to the table leg, to the seat of the chairs, brushes his pink nose, his white whiskers, across their surface, soft as a butterfly.

Under his chin, his belly, the top of his feet, there's a soft white fur: across his back, his tail, the top of his head, stripes of ginger darken and bronze in and out. When he reaches out one graceful paw to tap at the bookcase, we see the fleshy pink of his paw-pads, and we are enthralled. I had forgotten the delight of the paw-pads, their squashy plumpness.

Tom rolls him a small green plastic ball he's found in one of the bags. There's a bell inside this ball, and it jingles merrily across the tile floor over to Patrick, who observes it coolly. He looks up at us, and we look at each other, and think perhaps it's too soon, that he won't want to play, that it's all too new—but then there's a tinny burst as he taps the ball across the floor, as it skitters up against the sliding doors to the patio, and we smile at each other, relieved.

In the morning, as Tom readies himself for work, Patrick peeps round the doorframe and comes skulking low over the carpet and shoots under the bed, only to reappear on the other side almost immediately, a bright cork bobbing to the surface. He busies himself investigating the nightstand, nosing at the empty water glass, chewing thoughtfully for a moment on one of Tom's earplugs before I hastily retrieve it and shoo him off.

Tom tells me he'll give Patrick his breakfast and goes into the kitchen; I hear him exclaim as the cat weaves his way in and out of his legs, keeping close to his heels, as if herding a giant, laughing sheep.

I don't feel as bad as I have done the past week, but I'm drained, and moving around is an effort, my limbs stiff and uncooperative, any slight physical effort leaving a pale, sweaty sheen over my skin. My face looks sallow and moonish in the mirror, and I really should wash my hair, but I don't have the energy, so instead I put on a cardigan over my pajamas, and thick socks, and take my book out into the living room.

I lie under a blanket on the sofa and read. Patrick takes up his position on the top of the armchair opposite, stretching his front paws forwards in front of him, resting his head gently on top.

At some point I get up to make tea, and Patrick follows me into the kitchen, zigzagging ahead of my feet in their wooly socks. I tell him he can't have more food right now, and he gazes at me for a second; then, unperturbed, he laps quickly from the water bowl before following me back into the living room. This time he sits on the arm of the sofa I'm lying on, staring towards the window beyond; I get up and open the blinds slightly so he can watch the tree outside wave gently in the breeze and the occasional bird flit from branch to branch.

We will pass each morning that week this way, Patrick and I, and I will be struck again and again by how content I feel under my blanket, with my book and my socks and my tea, with this cat draped over the furniture, limbs hanging puppet-loose and lazy.

I'm an anxious sort, generally; swaths of unstructured time, tantalizing as they always seem beforehand, invariably end up leaving me feeling strangely paralyzed. With the time to do all the things I say I want to do, inevitably, I find myself doing none of them, instead wafting around rather uselessly, and, most frustrating of all, not even enjoying the not-doing-of-the-things. Feeling very bad, actually, about the not-doing-of-the-things. It wouldn't be all terrible if I could at least throw my hands in the air and announce I was officially going to do nothing but lie horizontally somewhere and read, or watch eighteen episodes of *Poirot* from 1994 back-to-back. I could at least enjoy myself doing nothing, then. But for some reason I can't quite work out, I never can make this declaration, can't quite sink into it and allow myself to enjoy it; instead, I rattle around feeling hollowed-out and empty, nerves ringing with guilt.

Being ill usually makes the anxiety worse. Once out of the sweating confusion of the feverish stage, my mind is clearer; clear enough to feel guilty for lying in bed or on the sofa, guilty that I am not working on the great list of things I've said I'll do and haven't done.

Today, however, this feeling, so familiar to me, is curiously absent. There is just me and my book and Patrick, and the sunlight drifting in through the slats in the blinds. I don't feel any pressing need to do anything much at all.

I'd forgotten how the presence of a cat can change a house, how a small creature can inhabit a space so utterly that you can feel the solidness of them as soon as you come in the door, even if they're lurking somewhere out of sight. It's a comfort, I remember now, as I watch Patrick watching the birds on the tree, his mouth twitching as he chirrups at them quietly. It's a comfort.

I'd had cats before, you see, in England.

First there'd been a black rescue, who had been researched online, visited at the Cats Protection League, adopted excitedly. Who'd grown old and tired and had died, curled like a comma, on the sofa in the house I'd shared with my ex, one bright June morning, a few days after my birthday.

It had all happened very quickly: she'd been really sick, thyroid problems causing her to shrink almost overnight, her sleek fur matting and clumping. The vet had said there wasn't much we could do; we'd been due to take her back the following day, but as it turned out, it was her time to leave us. Sick as she had been, I remember that the day before she died, she had taken herself out to sit in the garden, among the tiny blue flowers which winked out from the bed near the fence. She had lifted her little face to the sun. I have always believed she knew, somehow, and had wanted to smell the earth and the flowers and the trees one last time, to feel the warmth and the breeze on her fur.

We buried her in my ex's parents' garden, which overlooked acres of fields, where she could watch the rabbits and the deer come and go in the quiet of the morning, where she could watch the barn owls swoop, silent as velvet, when the moon rose in the sky.

I was devastated; we both were. I couldn't imagine having another, felt guilty at even the thought of it; she couldn't be replaced. The tiny house now seemed hugely empty; the silence was new, and deeper. It would not now be broken by a sleepy mew or padding feet.

I couldn't imagine another, but then, one day, my ex suggested a drive out into the countryside, out across the flat yellow of the fens, to a gray, pebble-dashed farmhouse, a car rusting in the yard outside, bikes leaning against the wall. From the house came a girl, no more than thirteen or so, holding out both arms. In each hand, a tiny, wriggling kitten. One, the larger, a tabby; the smaller—the runt, she told us—gray and white, with a pink nose, pink skin showing through the fine white fur on her ears.

Which one, she asked, and I realized why we were there. Of course we couldn't choose, not when we'd seen them both, seen their little pear-bellies and their tiny toes splaying out as they kneaded the air, and we took them both, those two tiny cats. Took them though I hadn't been ready, hadn't been prepared; took them anyway.

When it all ended, my ex took back the ring, the tiny house, the car, the TV, and half of our furniture, including the sofa on which our little black rescue had breathed her last. After, I had a tumbledown cottage in the woods which came with a new job at a boarding school. I had the battered green radio and the plates and bowls with chickens painted on them, the dining room table, some chairs.

And I had the two little cats.

I think, if I'm honest, that he'd been "their person." Cats usually have a favorite. They're quite ruthless that way. Now, however, I was all they'd got. And vice versa.

Now there were acres of time, despite my attempts to fill a good deal of my waking hours with work. There were hours and hours and hours in that house, enough time to list and to relist, endlessly, all my failings, all the missteps I'd made which had brought us all to this point. For a while, the mistakes weren't mine alone, I knew I had made many, and the memory of them thrummed through me like a pulse. I didn't expect to feel such a sense of failure, to feel it in the marrow of my bones, but I did. I felt if you cut me open, it'd be swirled through me, the failure, like the letters curling inside those striped candy sticks we'd buy from the fading English seaside towns of childhood summers. When it comes down to it, you see, we are all of us so capable of casual cruelties. I saw all of mine now, saw them clear-eyed, saw them all laid out, stark and ugly; and I was ashamed.

As we three settled into this new life of ours, the smallest cat took to following me up into my room at night, scurrying underneath the new bed my mother had helped me assemble from a flat-pack. Occasionally, I'd hear a chirrup or a scuffling sound, and she'd shoot out across the floor to attack a shadow on the skirting board or paw at one of the many water-marks under the paint on the walls. One morning, I leaned over to switch off my alarm and she slid out, on her back, as if on wheels, like a mechanic rolling out from under a car. I laughed out loud, and she brought her little legs up to the bed frame, turned her body so it lay parallel to the metal strut, and scooted herself along the carpet. Eventually, the sleeping under the bed became sleeping on the bed, curled up in a tight little ball, tail covering her eyes like a sleep mask. She wouldn't move at all when I got into bed, would simply ride the roll of the covers as my legs slid underneath as if she were a boat out on the tide. Sometimes I'd wake to find her nestled in between my shins, or laying alongside me, her little body stretched long as if she were leaping into the air.

The larger of the sisters, the tabby, was shy and less fond of sleeping on the bed or underneath it, although occasionally she would jump up in the mornings to have her head scratched behind her ear, just so. She did, however, like to perch, vigilant, on my nightstand, unnerving me when I opened my eyes in the morning to find her appraising me unblinkingly. Both of them liked to stick their whole heads into the glasses of water I'd bring up to bed, their faces contorted by the narrow space as they lapped at the water with their rough little tongues.

In the mornings on weekends, I liked to take my coffee and open the door to the garden and stand there looking out over the green and wet of the grass. Maintaining any semblance of order in the garden was mostly beyond me, and it soon became wild, with long-standing plants and trees growing tangled, the ivy covering the tall Victorian wall on one side thickening and darkening, the buddleia in front of the window growing tall enough to block out the light in the dining room. This was another thing I felt guilty about, the garden; occasionally someone from school would come and cut the lawn, trim the bushes back. Sometimes I'd hack at things with the puny shears I had found in a cupboard in an attempt to help, but mostly I would simply watch the birds come and go, the rabbits. A hedgehog, once, the cats sniffing at it, confused.

The cats would slink out from behind me like tigers, skulk through the long grass, wriggle and pounce on bugs, on butterflies. The Littlest, cute looking as she was, with her pink-tipped ears atop her tiny frame, was the fiercer hunter of the two, but they would both drag back all kinds of prey from the garden and the surrounding woods. Unfortunate rabbits, squirrels, birds, mice. Usually, they were quite dead, although there was a memorable occasion when I came back from work to find a baby rabbit, terrified but otherwise quite well, hiding in the living room, the larger of the sisters watching, puzzled on how best to proceed. The runt rarely left them alive, tiny assassin that she was. Another time, I was reading in bed when I heard that particular chirruping sound which inevitably announced the imminent deposit of some captured creature or other, and looked up to see Biggest chase in a mouse, who ran, squeaking bloody murder, across the carpet and under the nightstand.

The cats would come and sit by the bath when there was enough hot water from the aging boiler to fill the tub. They'd put their paws up on the rim and push their little faces towards mine, curious as to what I was doing there. Sometimes I'd play the radio and sing along; sometimes I'd read. They lost interest fairly quickly then. Other times, I'd simply lie there and watch the condensation form beads on the slope of the ceiling, study the mold speckling the plaster. Sometimes I'd cry, and the cats would look up at the sound of my snuffling, take up sentry positions atop the laundry basket.

I rattled around the hours in that house, feeling quite unsure as to how I was going to navigate this new reality of mine, and the cats were there, watching, licking their paws, twitching and curling the ends of their tails in greeting.

I spoke to them, of course. Bid them farewell in a cheery tone as I tripped out the door to work. I'd ask them what they intended to do with their furry little selves all day, told them I'd miss them. I spoke to them as I cooked, as I cleaned, as I got ready in the mornings, as I climbed into bed at night.

They were there, sitting on the counter, when I cried because I dropped my mug with the puffin on it, when I sobbed because after two years things still seemed so very, very hard, and now I'd broken my favorite cup with that plucky little bird on it and watched it smash into white splinters over the red tile of the kitchen floor.

They still came to nudge against my hand, purring, when I was guilty and worried because they wouldn't eat their worming tablets, no matter how much I tried to disguise them inside some tempting morsel or other, and I couldn't afford to buy more.

The Littlest didn't complain—too much—when I heaved her in the carrier by foot for over a mile to the vet, setting her down every few feet while I panted and huffed, because the presence of a new boyfriend had made her stressed and I couldn't afford a taxi to the surgery on top of the bill for her medicine.

They both came and curled themselves on the sofa when I sat there red-eyed after that same boyfriend turned out to be awful (the Littlest right all along).

Still, they came chirruping when I sat alone at the table over the bills I could not pay and wondered how long it would be like this, when I was angry because I'd been fed the idea by every song and every movie that surely after a time of difficulty would come a time of triumph, and it was looking, actually, like that was all a load of crap.

We find things only to lose them again, like shedding layers of skin. Find friends, find lovers, find purpose, identity; find security, find freedom; find beauty, find awe. Find joy. And we lose these things, too. Lose them through stubbornness or bad luck or poor choices, lose them sometimes for no reason at all.

For each of us a series of finding and losing. Of losing over and over until we think we can't take much more. But we can, and we do.

There are anchors, you see, that help us to hang on through the losses, to find ourselves again and again, to make even a tiny, shuffling progress through the days.

These anchors are the things so often overlooked, things which are ever constant, if not particularly flashy. The quiet of the garden. The sound of the birds. The solid warmth of a cat under your palm, its feet padding, happy and silent, towards you, day after day after day. Pulling us back into the present, to something solid. Giving us back ourselves. Here, you lost this, look; I've found it for you.

In time, there was another relationship, which teetered precariously along the edge of a time limit imposed by his job, by our nationalities. He'd be leaving, and what then?

For a long time, we didn't discuss it, not at all. The cats watched as I wrestled with it, this ticking clock, watched me turn it over and over and wonder what I was doing, what would happen.

Eventually, and not entirely expectedly, decisions were made. Plans were drawn up. I had a lot to do, because of course there was only one solution if we wanted to stay together, and it would mean packing up the cottage in the woods and leaving, not just the school but the town, the country—my country—and all that it contained.

I didn't want to think about it, but I knew, somewhere, that I wouldn't be able to bring them, my two little cats. I hadn't the money and wasn't sure they'd cope, didn't know where we'd end up. I had never taken on an animal only to give it up; I couldn't understand those who did; just thinking about it made my stomach churn and my throat tighten. I didn't think about it, if I could help it. I put it off, and I put it off, until a friend asked me gently what I was going to do.

In the end, I couldn't have asked for a better solution. I had a friend at work who had cats, who gave each of them voices; she narrated their adventures and regaled me with them in the staffroom over cups of tea. Her parents-in-law had lost their cat earlier in the year and, heartbroken, had not wanted another. But she'd been telling them about me, you see, and my two little cats, and—well—she thought they might be a good fit. They were retired, had a garden for them, had acres and acres of time to give them. They'd be so loved.

The week before he left, Tom and I hung out at my house the whole time, despite the heating that no longer worked and the shower which didn't run more than a trickle. We watched movies on DVD because I'd already shut off the internet, and he took photographs of them, my two little cats, on his camera. Photographs of them crouching by the window chirruping at the birds, photographs of them curled up tight as sea fossils, photographs of me holding them, tearful, smiling.

He left the country before I did, and so my best friend came that last day. I was worried because the Littlest had disappeared outside, and there'd been times before when both of them had sauntered off into the woods and not appeared for days, despite my frantic searching and calling and stapling up of posters. I was due to leave the next day, for good. What if she didn't return? What then?

We'd already coaxed the Biggest into her carrier, and she sat there looking at us, expecting the vet, I suppose. I was already crying. I couldn't find the little one anywhere, and I went into the garden, called for her, my voice catching with sobs. I went out the front of the house and into the woods, like I'd done before, to no avail, when she'd gone off. I called out, over and over, but there was nothing, just as there'd been nothing those times before: just the trees and the sky and the occasional grating call of a rook.

I stood there a moment, my chest heaving up and down, and I called again, a half-strangled sort of sound. There was a rustling, and I turned, and there she was, the Littlest, her tiny gray and white body hurtling through the green towards me: I'd found her. She'd found me. I picked her up and held her to my chest, and for once she didn't wriggle too much but lay still and quiet against me as my heart hammered underneath her, as the tears rolled in great hot splashes down my face and onto her fur.

My friend from work had arrived, was smiling and gentle: she understood. Her boys were excited to see the cats, excited to take them to their new home at their grandparents' house. I stood with my best friend and watched as they drove away, my two little cats in their carriers I'd brought them home in as babies.

Did they understand? Did they know how I loved them?

I couldn't bear the thought that they might think I'd give them up easily, as the soil gives up buried bones under the plough, yielding and silent. I couldn't bear the idea they'd be looking for me, thinking I was lost, wondering where to find me. I stood in the drive and I hoped, more than anything, that somehow they knew, that somehow they understood.

When I think of them now, those two little cats of mine, as I lie on the sofa, thousands of miles away, my throat tightens; there's a familiar ache, a cord knotting tight. I lie there and Patrick comes and sits next to me, his solid weight warm against mine. I stroke his head and he purrs.

This man who was my boyfriend will be my husband, and we will leave this place soon and travel to another. In that change, inevitably, will come loss.

I stroke Patrick's head, look at his little pink paws.

My friend sent me pictures of my two little cats. They are fat and happy. Littlest sitting in a flower pot, Biggest sleeping on a sofa. I know that they are loved, madly.

I hope they understood, somehow, this parting, this loss. I hope they can understand what they meant to me, my tiny furry anchors, how they brought me back to myself, over and over again. How they helped me to find what was lost.

Patrick purrs and stretches. He's asleep now, completely limp. And I see that there could be another cat, for me, for us. I see that we can find another friend to bring into our home. That it will be okay to do that. That there will always be loss, because loss, you see, is all woven up with love. I loved, I did my best; I failed just as many times as I won.

I lost, but I loved anyway. I love anyway.

A GOOD CAT IS HARD TO FIND

Jackie Soro

A GOOD CAT IS HARD TO FIND

1. AS A LESBIAN, I OPERATE IN A VERY CAT-CENTERED CULTURE.

2. I LOVE CATS.

3. I AM QUITE ALLERGIC TO CATS.

3A. AS SUCH, IT BECOMES
    NECESSARY FOR ME
TO KEEP ANTIHISTAMINES
IN MY CAT-LOVING LOVERS'
    HOMES.

I LOVE YOU BUT ACHOO.

4. CAT LESBIANS
   ARE PREFERRABLE TO
   DOG LESBIANS.[1,2]

---

footnotes:

1. IN THE END, DOG LESBIANS WILL
   CHOOSE THEIR CANINE PARTNER(S)
   OVER YOU.
2. DOG LESBIANS GET UP TOO EARLY.

5. I HAVE MET THE
   PERFECT CAT.
HER NAME IS GOLDIE
AND SHE LIVES IN
      UPSTATE NEW YORK.

FIG 5a.
GOLDIE LAYING
PROVOCATIVELY ON THE FLOOR.

6. I HAVE NOT MET THE
PERFECT LOVER.
- I HAVE LOOKED
- I'LL KEEP LOOKING
- MORALE IS LOW

7. I LIED. A GOOD CAT IS
NOT HARD TO FIND, THEY'RE
EVERYWHERE.

8. THIS FAR INTO QUARATINE
I'D RATHER HAVE A CAT,
I THINK, THAN A LOVER.

NB. :
EITHER WAY
A WARM BODY
WOULD BE
NICE.

JUNE
2020

TAKE A CAT WALK WITH US

Katie Haegele, graphics by Joe Carlough

I've always loved to go for long walks in the city, and the suburbs and the woods sometimes, too. Moving my body through space and taking in some new sights always, always makes me feel good, or at least better than I felt before I started.

During the quarantines of 2020, however, walking came to mean way more to me. Since it was one of the only things I felt safe doing outside of my house, I leaned *all* the way in. Bored? Go for a walk. Taking a break from work? Go for a walk. Need to talk something out with Joe? Go for a walk—with Joe. Though actually, all of these walks have been with Joe. Everything I did during the pandemic, I did with him. I'm not tired of his company, I'm very happy to say, and I haven't gotten bored of our walks yet, either.

However, quarantine fatigue is a real phenomenon, and some days the stress of it all pressed down on us more heavily than others. We found it useful to mix things up here and there. On one of these walks—as we talked about how we hoped we'd see Seamus, the large, majestic creature with long fur who we sometimes see framed in the front window of the stately house where he lives, surveying the street like an old fisherman staring out to sea (hence the Irish nickname we gave him)—the thought occurred to us: we should start keeping track of every cat we see. These little cat-finding missions really invigorated our neighborhood walks, let me tell you. For one thing, they encouraged me to pay a kind of attention to the visual details around me that I tend to miss when I'm looking down at my feet, lost in my thoughts. It's hard to stay preoccupied with worry when you're scanning the scenery around you, hoping to spot a cat. There's something comical about this particular project, too, and it brought a note of joy to the walks that we really needed, some days more than others. The cats are funny, and coming upon them in the middle of their activities is funny, too.

There's the gray cat that was lying so sound asleep in the grass of its front yard that I swore it was a large rock until we crossed the street to get a better look, and it stood up, stretched, and yawned. There's the big orange tabby we sometimes see in his front door, where he sits happily on a cat tower that his humans have placed there. As we pass by, we watch him and he watches us. Sometimes we'll really luck out and see Ozzy, the pretty gray and black tabby who has only ever been seen on a leash, being walked by his owner, a man in maybe his thirties who is so extremely shy or private or something that he constantly watches movies on his phone while he's out on his walks so he won't have to look up and say hello to the people, like us, who want to make a fuss over his cat. We know the cat's name because he apparently poops in people's gardens sometimes, so he's been the subject of some discussion on our neighborhood's petty Facebook group. Joe and I don't care about any of that, and we're quietly respectful of the duo whenever we pass them. The last time we saw them, chilling on the steps of the church as we huffed and puffed our way up the hill, Ozzy's guy gave us a little head nod, and we felt blessed.

Keeping track of the cats on our walks has given us a new appreciation for just how much is happening in our corner of the world. There's a lot of *life* in a city neighborhood, even when it's been hemmed in by a pandemic: cats in windows, people tending to their window-box gardens, a random laugh from the basketball court, a tree full of chirpy birds. Undertaking a small, dorky project like this can be really life-affirming, and I'm glad we were able to remember that during this time of endless boredom and fear.

When we get home from our walks we tally up our results in a spreadsheet Joe made. (Joe loves making spreadsheets.) Date, time of day, number of cats spotted indoors, number of cats spotted outdoors, and any useful notes. ("Saw a round boi on his back patio"; "Three black cats on this October day!") For publication in this book, Joe has helpfully arranged some of our data into charts and graphs. We don't know yet who will find the information we're compiling most useful—urban planners? cat behavioral scientists?—but we are glad to be here, collecting it.

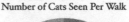

Cats Per Time of Day

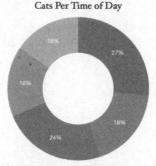

- Morning (8-11am)
- Early Evening (5-7:30pm)
- Midday (11-2pm)
- Evening (7:30-10pm)
- Afternoon (2-5pm)

Number of Cats Seen Per Walk

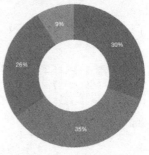

- 0-4
- 5-9
- 10-14
- 15-19

Cats Per Time of Day	
Morning (8-11am) - 6 walks	45
Midday (11-2pm) - 5 walks	31
Afternoon (2-5pm) - 6 walks	40
Early Evening (5-7:30pm) - 4 walks	27
Evening (7:30-10pm) - 2 walks	26
Total Cats Seen	169

Number of Cats Seen Per Walk	
0-4	7
5-9	8
10-14	6
15-19	2

Analysis: In the time between September 16 and November 4, we observed 169 cats throughout our neighborhood: 82 inside houses, 87 outside. We've found Time of Day (ToD) is an important factor; cats seem to be most actively found during the morning and evening. We theorize the cats are most active around their humans waking and relaxing together after work. We look forward to taking more evening walks to level out the data. As we begin to walk more regularly, we will accumulate a new data set of the cats we see most regularly.

Analysis: At an average rate of 7.347826087 cats seen per walk, our rate of seeing cats has remained consistent only in its consistency. Perhaps due to the mercurial nature of cats, it's difficult to predict when we will see the most cats. We do, however, have some favorites we see often: the calico cat on Sunnyside, the tabby in the window on Stanton, and the kitten of St. Bridget's. We have now tied for a "high score" of 17 cats: on 10/15/2020 at 5 p.m, and on 10/25/2020 at 10:15 a.m. Perhaps ToD isn't as important to the statistics as once thought, but that should become more apparent as we apply more datasets.

Cats We've Seen

September 16 to November 4

CATS PER WALK

CATS (INDOOR LINES / OUTDOOR DOTS)

AVERAGE CATS (AC)	AVERAGE INDOOR CATS (AIC)	AVERAGE OUTDOOR CATS (AOC)
7.35	**3.57**	**3.78**
TOTAL CATS (TC)	MOST CATS AT ONCE (MCAO)	LEAST CATS AT ONCE (LCAO)
169.00	**17.00**	**1**

WALK_ID	DATE	TIME OF DAY	INDOOR CATS	OUTDOOR CATS	TOTAL CATS
W1	9/16/20	8:30 AM	2	3	5
W2	9/18/20	8:30 AM	8	6	14
W3	9/22/20	12:30 PM	0	1	1
W4	9/23/20	7:00 PM	6	8	14
W5	9/28/20	9:00 AM	2	2	4
W6	10/4/20	10:30 AM	1	3	4
W7	10/5/20	6:00 PM	6	4	10
W8	10/7/20	7:30 PM	1	6	7
W9	10/8/20	4:30 PM	8	3	11
W10	10/9/20	3:30 PM	1	4	5
W11	10/11/2020	10:00 AM	0	1	1

Our charts account for only a few months' worth of data and we're far from finished compiling it. I mean, just the other day a house across the street got two kittens, and the last time we went out for a walk, we spotted them sitting side by side, each framed by its own window, looking out at us with the same daffy expression of wonderment on their faces. A surprising, hilarious sighting, life being affirmed yet again. Remembering about the kittens now, it occurs to me that things in our neighborhood will just keep changing, cat-wise. Our work may never be finished!

CLOVER

Kelsey Stewart

I grew up in a row home in the City of Reading, Pennsylvania. Our house was narrow, but not too skinny, and it fit our family of six like a cozy sweater, snug with a little extra room, but not too much of it. There were lots of good secret spots in that little house. There was the coat closet, where if you dived deep enough you'd find my dad's old accordion and a pair of high heels that didn't belong to anyone in our family; a big deep closet in the attic that housed love letters written by my parents in the seventies; and a small nook closet, with its tiny metal twist knob, that was big enough to sit in with a flashlight and a book, if you didn't mind the smell of mothballs.

Of all the good secret spots, our basement was the biggest. It was crammed with photos and books, old cups and board games, and whatever else we didn't have a home for upstairs, but also didn't have the heart to discard.

It housed so many years of keepsakes that to get from one end of our basement to the other, a small path had been cleared. The path was, conveniently, the width of a laundry basket. Our basement was like a mood ring that understood the wearer's needs, and it shape-shifted accordingly. When my siblings and I needed a playplace, we'd travel the path to its end in order to attend a make-believe school, complete with a chalkboard, bench, and writing assignments. For my father, the basement became an at-home gym where he could work out on the NordicTrack or hang on the Upside Down machine for a while. And for my mother, like most spaces, it became a garden oasis, a makeshift greenhouse where she'd pile cardboard boxes precariously on top of bins, on top of folding tables, so that her small plants could reach the delicious fluorescent light and grow.

On days that were too snowy to get down our front stairs, the basement served as a secret passageway into our neighbor's house so we could visit without putting on a snowsuit. When we started to experience break-ins, we locked our basement doors with deadbolts, and once we found dusty footprints of the person who broke into our house, stomped from the crawl space onto my dad's black weight bench, down the skinny path, and frantically back out again.

So, seven years into living in Philadelphia, when my mother called to tell me that she and my father thought a feral cat from the neighborhood was lost in their house and taking refuge in the basement, it didn't surprise me.

"We know one got in, we're just not sure where he is," she said nonchalantly into the phone before moving on to other pressing subjects, like new diets and what songs my father had covered the previous evening at an open-mic night. For a few weeks, that was the last I heard of the feral cats of Fourth Street.

When I visited Reading at the end of that summer, I noticed the couch had been replaced with plastic lawn furniture, and wondered if that had anything to do with cat piss.

"Is there still a cat in here?" I asked, kicking off my flip-flops a bit more cautiously than usual.

"We think he got out again," my dad answered. "The neighborhood is overrun with cats these days, but to be honest, it isn't the worst problem to have. We haven't seen mice in a long time. Want to go on our run?"

Every time I go home, my father and I run together in the cemetery at the top of our block. We run laps on the paths that circle both the old and the new graves, while enjoying the shade of the cemetery's trees and each other's company.

When we were back home from the run, I stepped out onto the porch to cool down. I sat on the top step, sipping water and looking up and down our block, seeing what had changed and what had stayed the same over the years. Suddenly, a large-pawed, gray cat approached. I jumped up and ran inside the house. Squished between the screen door and our wooden door, I could hear my dad laughing from the plastic loveseat as I eyed the cat. Was he feral or was he friendly?

That's just Clover. He's not going to hurt you. He's a very nice cat.

Clover? Who named him that?

The Block named him.

I got to know Clover. He was a sweet, soft cat, despite his outdoor life. He had a knack for approaching unseen and unheard. Over the next year, whenever I visited home, he'd come visit me on the porch. Once, I saw him across the street, strutting from the roof of one car to the next, like he was a character singing a solo in a musical. He walked with such an air of comfortability on Fourth Street that it felt like he'd always been there.

And then, on one visit, he was gone. I didn't see him slipping by in the shadow of the cars, or sleeping in the shade of the alleyways, and I missed him. Something about the way Clover had accepted me so quickly into the landscape of the neighborhood resonated with me. It made me feel like he knew I belonged there, even if I was only there every couple of months or so. I asked my dad if he'd seen him, and he said he hadn't. Not for a while. My dad thought Clover had been adopted into a house somewhere, since he was such a sweetheart.

I really hope Clover and his big paws found a good spot.

SKY

Keet Geniza

Sky

Ever since I saw him walking by, I've been dying to meet him.

His name was Skyler and he lived across the street.

I finally did at a party. He went right up to me and took a nap at my feet. He was perfect.

He liked to remind people that the couch was his domain. He would climb up the armrest and waited until you pet him.

Sky and I were polite with each other. Though I liked cats, I'm not used to them, so I can't really tell if he liked me or not.

"Dear Ms. Advice Columnist, I really like this cat. How do I know if he likes me?"

"If he meets you at the door hangs out near your feet when you visit, that's a sign that he does, right?"

One time at yet another holiday party, he ignored me all night. I was depressed at the time so I took it personally.

On his way up to bed, though, he paused in front of me for a long, long time.

I knew if I pet him everything would've been alright.

I ignored him.

We didn't see each other for a year after that.

Last spring, we were invited to dinner. He wasn't at the door.

Um... Where's Sky?

I think he forgave me.

Hey ♥

REST IN PEACE, BUDDY.

REQUIEM FOR BELOVED SKUKL QUEEN OF THE NIGHT

Justin Duerr

KING OF THE NEIGHBORHOOD

Joe Biel

*I*n 2008 I was homeless, living on a friend's couch, when I began working on a new feature documentary film. When one of my interview subjects flaked, I ran into Elly and interviewed her instead.

Elly and I first met back in 2005 at city hall, when she bought a T-shirt from me and I tried to flirt with her, ignoring the name of her partner on the check she paid with. A few years later, she called me to get some stickers, but I was dating someone else at the time and again, our transaction was all business.

So I was a little surprised in 2009 when she began showing up at my office and at the friend's house whose couch I slept on. I got eye surgery that year and was incapacitated for a few weeks, and she showed up with food and was mysteriously familiar with my diet. Soon, she was putting in my eye drops, and before long, I had recovered and was staying at the same place where she was staying.

The time to think about cohabitation was nigh.

Trying to take advantage of Portland's last affordable housing option, I planned to build a tiny house on a trailer frame for us to live in. Elly said that her ex, John, had a trailer frame he'd intended to use for a food cart, but it wasn't sturdy enough. I biked over there to take a look. A handful of cats greeted me and, in fact, seemed to manage the property with a style befitting the Three Musketeers. They chased each other around, hid behind doorways, and took swipes at each other. Elly told me that the youngest cat was named Tigger.

Tigger had belonged to an elderly neighbor who had adopted the cat for his granddaughter. The four-year-old, under some apparent influences, named the cat. Problem was, Grandpa decided that the cat could live in the garage and outdoors, but Tigger, if he is anything, is a bit of a vain prince, and a garage corner is not befitting of royalty. The cat began visiting Elly and

John, and finding food, shelter, and a domicile, he decided to move in. Elly and John eventually had an awkward conversation with Tigger's previous owner, who happily relieved himself of the cat that he didn't want. Later, when Elly moved out, the cats seemed to grieve the failed relationship more than anyone else involved. Whenever she visited after that, Tigger would position himself like a military general on her bike seat and plead with her not to leave.

A year or so after all of this, a book I published became a runaway bestseller. Within months, I realized that I should stop spending the money impulsively and might instead consider the possibility that Elly and I would probably not want to spend the rest of our lives in the 98 square feet of our travel trailer. Within three months, we'd found our current home, tucked away on my dream street in my favorite neighborhood in the city, within walking distance from the apartment where I had stayed during my first few months in Portland in the '90s. It was like a little cottage, too small for a family and with nowhere to park a car, but in the most desirable school district on the east side. It was fancier than anywhere else I'd ever lived, with a dishwasher, white picket fence, new bamboo floors, and a fresh kitchen remodel.

Naturally, Elly wasted no time broaching the subject about adding a third resident. I agreed, and she biked to John's to negotiate the terms of Tigger's release. John was hesitant, but Tigger had made it apparent that he was the one picking on the other cats. His playful kitten antics had revealed themselves to be a bit more incendiary than they'd first appeared. John agreed that Tigger could move if Elly put a collar on the cat, failing, perhaps, to remember that Tigger calls the shots.

During his first week in our new house, Tigger hid under the bed, then under the covers, then finally on top of the covers. He would panic if I tried to pet him. Little did we know, these were the first stages of his slowly growing his territory. Elly put a collar on him, but each day the cat would remove it. Eventually, fed up with the suggestion that someone else might be humorously engaged in a power struggle with him, Tigger hid the collar, and we never saw it again.

You see, the collar had gotten in the way of Tigger's one and only habit: eradicating other creatures that wandered into his domain. If a cat exists within a few blocks of our house, Tigger chases it off. If the cat doesn't flee, Tigger does his best impression of *The Warriors* meets *Game of Thrones*. And if he ever finds a bird or mouse, he'll proudly present it to Elly . . . who promptly recoils in horror at the bloody, half-dead decomposition.

After he successfully removed all the other cats on our block, we watched as Tigger's territory expanded across busy city streets. If we take a walk, Tigger will follow. It can be hard to tell if he's curious about our whereabouts or just reminding us that he still runs the show. We've worried that Tigger would continue his housing upgrade scheme by adopting a family with even greater resources, but instead, he simply adopts other families and houses during the day while we are at work, only to run across the street when he hears us coming home, presumably for a second dinner.

Despite his imperialist tendencies, Tigger is not always a cruel dictator. It's unclear if he has begun to rest on his laurels or if he's just removed every threat, no matter how insignificant, to his throne. When we have guests, he merely curls up in the most choice lap and begins purring. He will cheerfully displace the book you're reading or plant himself on your keyboard. He is most comfortable on my chest or head while I'm sleeping, but when we wake up in the morning, he'll already have quietly slinked outside, hoping for a chance to purge his territory of rivals. At five in the morning, his internal alarm clock sounds, and he climbs in through the back door to begin demanding his breakfast.

As far as overlords go, it's a tenable relationship, and one that leaves us inclined to overlook any inconveniences in favor of the positive endorphins he leaves in his wake.

SPRING, AT HOME

Joe Carlough, illustration by Mocha Ishibashi

On the first day of Spring
we raise all the blinds
we throw open the windows
we open all of the doors
and let the fresh, cool air
course through the house
like the house is breathing

my cat closes her eyes

inhales deeply
exhales deeply

I imitate her and do the same

and for a moment
we are again a part
of the same ecosystem

GRANDMA FINEGOLD AND BOO BOO KITTY OR PRINCESS

Rachel Blythe Udell and Jeremy Newman

THE STORY OF MR. CAT

Amanda Laughtland

*A*s baby kittens, Mr. Cat and his sister lived in the care of an animal rescue organization. The daughters in the family who fostered them called the cats Bart and Bijou. When my former partner Trish adopted the cats, she named them Midnight and Shadow. They were small enough to squeeze under her bathroom door when she was at work, so she had to change tack so they wouldn't fall down the stairs.

Mr. Cat has a sleek black coat with one barely noticeable spot of white under his chin. His sister was soft and gray, a Russian blue; she developed cancer and died when she was eight. Mr. Cat is twelve now and has some trouble with arthritis, but when he came to stay with me a few months ago, I made a mistake in assuming at first he didn't want to play. Now, he has a toy like a tiger's tail on a string, and sometimes he claws it and other times sleeps with it.

Mr. Cat is called Midnight at the vet's office and by people who always call everyone by their official names and would never accept that his name could actually be Mr. Cat. I still call him Midnight sometimes, but I think of him as Mr. Cat. He just has become known that way.

The story of Mr. Cat becoming Mr. Cat goes back to the original Mr. Cat, whose official name was Tiger. Tiger was Trish's sister's cat until Trish's mom and dad started having trouble with mice, and Tiger came to visit and help out and then never went back to Trish's sister's house. Something like ten years ago, when Trish and I went on a road trip to visit her parents in Denver, I met Rosie O'Grady the dog, and the original Mr. Cat.

I asked about the name, and Trish's mom, Barb, said, "I decided he was a cat who needed a title, so I call him Mr. Cat."

At the time, Barb ran a small daycare in her basement, and she had written a letter to the daycare parents in the voice of Rosie, explaining Rosie's tendency to bark and how Rosie took it as her job to protect the kids. "Thanks for understanding," Barb/ Rosie had signed the letter.

After we got home to Seattle, Trish and I kept "thanks for understanding" in our regular vocabulary, and we started to refer to Midnight as Mr. Cat. Didn't he need a title, too? Shadow already held herself like a cat who had a title; we sometimes called her Baby Cat because she was a lot smaller than her brother (and quite a bit tougher).

Mr. Cat came to stay with me in June of 2021, when Trish was getting ready for a couple of summer trips. He stayed here last summer for a time, too, but then went back to her place. For some reason, this year he really settled in.

"How's Mr. Cat?" my dad asks when he stops by, and Mr. Cat comes and sits between us on the couch.

"Hi, Mr. Cat," my mom says when she visits, continuing to pet him, "As long as you don't sit on my lap," as she reminds him, which he doesn't because he's a next-to cat rather than a lap cat.

I asked Trish last week if she wanted him to come back to her place. She misses him but says he's happy at my house and that it's been easier not worrying about him as she continues to train her very large dog, Okie, a Great Pyrenees she found two summers ago while taking Barb on a road trip to Oklahoma.

Barb made up a song about Okie to the tune of "Beautiful Dreamer": "Beautiful puppy, I love you so / Beautiful puppy, from Oklahomo." Nobody has written a song about Mr. Cat, but I don't think he minds. As I was finishing this story, he turned up to sit next to me and wash his face. He's a handsome gentleman indeed.

CATS IN DRAWERS, STUDY #6

Nicholas Beckett

meow...

Smokey?

Puuu

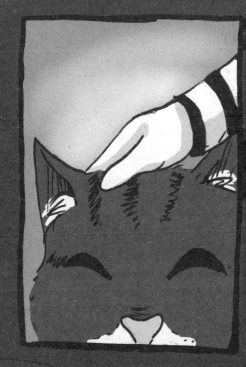

I'm still alive

W.What?

GASP

I'm still alive...

88

You were never there.

CATTY

Alison Lee Chapman

*T*he year after my father died, my sister rescued a
kitten from drowning in a flooded window well.
She brought it to my parents' house, where it hid
under the furniture for weeks. My mom didn't know
if we were keeping it or if my sister would find it a new home.
We figured it would stay, at least for a while, because who wants
a kitten that's afraid of the world? So we left food and water
nearby and waited for it to come out.

I had moved back to my parents' house to stay for a while, unsure of how long. Life without my dad seemed vast, in that terrifying, gasping way—like treading water in the middle of the ocean. In the wake of my dad's passing, my childhood home was one of those aftershock blankets you'd get in the back of an ambulance, something to cling to that's life affirming. I couldn't find peace anywhere else.

As I milled through my days, the cat ventured out from hiding, lurking around my bedroom. She would sit on the windowsill, enjoying the sunshine from her safe space, occasionally looking in my direction, blinking slowly.

I called her Catty, a joke based on her spiteful disposition. She tolerated a few tender moments here and there, allowing a minute or two of chin scratches until she decided that it was enough, and she would abruptly sulk away.

I couldn't blame her for the way she was; her earliest memories are of almost dying. I'm not sure traumatized cats can force optimism upon themselves, and I'm not sure they should, either. Optimism doesn't help small animals stay alive.

Eventually, I enrolled in art school in Philadelphia. I hated leaving my mom's house and leaving Catty behind. But in forcing optimism upon myself, I had decided that this was the right step towards something like moving forward. Catty had gotten braver too, taking short ventures into the yard. I watched her courage grow as she tentatively explored the tall grasses behind the house.

Some time after I moved, my mom told me that Catty had gone out all the way into the woods and hadn't come back. I waited for news of her eventual return, but the news never came.

Had Catty gone looking for me? Was I the only thing that kept her at the house? Or had she even noticed I was gone?

Who knows how long she survived out there, in full view of hawks and coyotes. It's possible that her hiding skills and mistrust of every living thing kept her alive longer than the average escaped house pet. Maybe she lived fifteen more years, a silent hunter, a ghost of the forest. A survivor.

I still keep my eye out for her when I visit home. It's been almost twenty years, though—so now when I walk through those woods, I imagine her spirit, an apparition, darting between thickets along the forest's edge. For every dead field mouse carcass I come across, I wonder if it's her making an offering from the afterlife.

I tell her, wherever she is, that I'm sorry I left. I am sorry if her adventures led to her being carried off, full of fear, to the end of her life.

But I'm not sorry if when she left, she thrived, unburdened and finally unafraid.

LUMINOUS BEINGS

Mardou

*M*y first psychic encounter with a feline was with my then-boyfriend's cat, a scruffy, scrawny former stray named Soldy, of indeterminate age. She was, incidentally, the first cat I ever loved, though she wasn't especially lovable right off the bat. She had dandruff, missing teeth, would eat wet food off her grody little paws and then not groom herself afterwards. And she had this persistent green-snot drip dangling from her nostril after a lingering respiratory infection. The vet just shrugged. I did some herbalist research and tried lacing her Fancy Feast with goldenseal tincture and it actually worked. I'd wipe her little paws clean after every meal and, being unemployable (no green card yet), spent long days at home with her. We grew to love each other, this old cat and I.

One time, I was looking into Soldy's green-gold eyes and in my mind told her that I loved her. She held my gaze, and I swear she sent a wordless love-whump feeling right back at me. I felt it tingle in my forehead.

I don't know. I'm not saying the experience had mystic value or anything, but I do think at the very least some degree of telepathy is a natural, mostly unused gift of humans and some animals too. The renegade scientist Rupert Sheldrake in his book *Dogs That Know When Their Owners Are Coming Home*, told this story about his own cat, Allegra:

"She was out at night, since my attempts to call her in before I went to bed had failed. At about 3:00 a.m., my wife, Jill, suddenly woke up and saw Allegra's face pressed very close to her own, looking her in the eyes. But the cat was not there. She tried to get back to sleep but could not, and after about a quarter of an hour, she got out of bed and went downstairs to find Allegra's face pressed against the glass of the French windows waiting to come in."

It doesn't seem so odd to me, telepathy between mammals who like each other. My husband and I have often had dream telepathy as well as the daytime variety. Once, he was in Texas on a trip, I was home in St. Louis, we both dreamed of tiny cats. Another time, most inexplicably, in 2005, we both dreamed of Helen Mirren. She hadn't come up in the news or in conversation and we were on opposite sides of the Atlantic at the time. Call it the playful universe or whatever you want, but it seemed a little too specific and weird to be just chance.

Well, my cat-love Soldy died in 2008. She was very old; it was a swift, unmedicated ending. In her final minutes, she lay in my arms, taking far-apart rasping breaths until the lights in her eyes went out. It was my first and, so far, only direct experience of death.

We didn't get another cat for a long time. Three years later, I was looking at Facebook and some friend, a crazy-cat-person type, shared an animal shelter's death row roundup post. Maybe you know the thing: "Unless adopted, all these cats will be euthanized on Thursday at 1:00 p.m." I clicked, telling myself not to click, and immediately saw a photo of this unfriendly looking calico. She looked too much like Soldy to pass on. That was my girl. We got her on Wednesday.

The first night home with us, she was surprisingly confident, this New Cat. Watchful, timid, but curious about us and not hiding.

It took three tries to figure out her name. My then three-year-old daughter (a big fan of *Gumby* at the time) suggested the name Dondo (admittedly it did sound like an Art Clokey sort of name). But no! I stepped in and suggested Donna as being a more appropriate variation. My husband was quite firm: "You can't call a cat Donna!" and countered with Connie. At which this friendly, watchful cat piped up and mewed as if in recognition.

"Connie, is your name Connie?" we asked. And yes, sure enough. She mewed her affirmation many more times. The cat chose the name, we tell people, and it's true. She comes padding into the room like a lazy little puppy whenever you call her name out.

Shortly after that first night's christening, I had a dream about her. In this dream, Connie could talk to me, in a small, "whurry" kind of voice. "So what's your true name?" my dream self asks, and she answers "Pharaoh."

Whoa! That's far-out, my dream self thought, but then it occurred to me that she might mean "Faro," like the whole-grain cereal. So I ask again, "Wait, do you mean Pharaoh like the Egyptian kings or Faro like the cereal?" But she just looks at me and repeats "Pharaoh." Or Faro.

In real life, Connie would make a good temple cat. She comes and sits by our zazen pillows whenever we meditate. So for that reason, I'm going with Pharaoh.

When my daughter turned seven, she wanted a kitten more than anything in the world. "But," she sighs, "I know I have to wait for Connie to 'go bleugh.'" To 'go bleugh' is to die; the idea of death is distasteful to my daughter, and she won't say the actual d-word. I vaguely agreed and changed the subject. But the idea took hold of me. I am really quite keen on cats now, and a kitten? Well, my own childhood was unhappy, and here I am at 42, my life is full of love, and I want my kid to be the kind of person who looks back on her childhood and remembers joy. If she wants a kitten so bad, well . . . why not?

It has pretty much ruined Connie's existence. Mimi, the rescue kitten, was just ten weeks old and a calico (of course). She looks even more like Soldy than Connie does. Those early days were magical. She'd play until she was exhausted and then fall asleep in my daughter's arms. We were all enchanted.

It didn't last long. My curtains have holes in them; treasured ornaments have been knocked off of high shelves and smashed. Houseplants have been chewed. Glasses of water have been knocked over piles of library books. The sofa is her scratching post, and we've caught her chewing on electric cords. Oh my god, what have we done? It's too much.

Honestly, I can't stand her mostly.

"We can't yell at her, we just have to be firm and consistent," I repeat, trying not to yell at her. But then one day, I walk into the room and she's chewing on a philodendron leaf, this beautiful once-huge plant that is almost dead, and I lose my cool. I yell. Mimi runs off, squirming under the sofa, but I grab her flank, scoop her up angrily, yelling "No, no" and tap her on the rump, sharply. Mimi, in a panicked fit, freaks out, wriggles, and twists her neck to sink her teeth briefly into my wrist. And as I cry in pain, she looks me hard in the eyes—a flash between us—

Oh god, she's just a baby, growing into herself, why am I being so harsh to her? I toss her as gently as I can into my daughter's bedroom and close the door. Wash my wrist and look deeply at myself in the bathroom cabinet mirror before opening to reach for the Neosporin.

I'm glad she bit me; I saw her soul for a moment . . .

There's a quote I read by the Buddhist teacher Ajahn Chah, it goes like this: "The rumors and teachings are true: we are luminous beings and awakening is our nature." (I'm pretty sure he said it before Yoda did.)

I bring it up here because it touches upon a sort of restless longing I feel these days. It's why I meditate and practice yoga and pay attention to dreams and telepathy and all that herbalism stuff . . . I want to feel my own inner light, I guess. And to learn to see that light in others. Really see it.

I just know that being with a cat makes me feel a little closer to this nameless quality I'm looking for. They too are little luminous beings. I know it!

KITTEN SOCKS

Ally Shwed

THIS IS **SCHNEIDER.**

HE ALSO GOES BY BREAD, LITTLE ONE, AND ITTY BITTY.

HE'S A CHATTY FELLOW, AND SOMETIMES, HE SQUEAKS.

SQUEAK

HE LIKES HOCKEY AND FOOTBALL. HE'S A FAN OF THE DEVS AND THE JAGS.

HE RUNS A BREWERY CALLED KITTEN SOCKS. THEY ONLY BREW PILSNERS.

HE TRIED HIRING HIS BROTHER EGON.

BUT EGON SEES GHOSTS, AND IT INTERFERED WITH HIS WORK.

HE ALSO ONCE TRIED MAKING A GARLIC PILSNER. IT DIDN'T TURN OUT WELL.

HE DOES IMPRESSIONS. HIS FAVORITE IS KERMIT THE FROG SAYING "YAAAAYY", LIKE ON *THE MUPPET SHOW.*

BOO!

A POEM
BY MELLEN REINBOLD

A SHADOW IN THE CORNER, JUST BEYOND MY PERIPHERAL
A SHAPE-SHIFTING RAIN CLOUD WITH GLOWING YELLOW EYES.
YOUR VOICE LIKE RAIN, YOUR PRESENCE - RAUCOUS THUNDER
BITTER SWEETNESS WHEN I SWEAR I HEAR YOUR CRIES.

JUST ONE MORE TIME
I HOPE TO KNOW YOUR COMFORT.
JUST ONE MORE TIME
I HOPE TO SEE YOUR FACE.
YOU WERE WITH ME THROUGH SO MUCH
AND YET IT'S CLEAR NOW.
I MUST STILL GO ON
WITHOUT YOU IN THIS PLACE.

YOU HAD A GENTLE HUM THAT CHASED AWAY MY SADNESS.
FROM THE CORNER OF MY EYES, I STILL SEE YOU.
A FAMILIAR PRESENCE WAITS SOMEWHERE BEYOND HERE.
A FRIENDLY LITTLE CAT, THAT I CALLED BOO.

RIP 2007-2020

KITTENS AND COCKTAILS

Raymond E. Mingst

My handshake is neither limp nor crushing. It is firm. My posture is good. One doesn't eat food while walking down the street, nor would you comb your hair while out in public. These are some of the lessons my parents taught me. The ones I remember best were those taught earliest, perhaps when I was about five years old. I appreciated knowing how to be in society, the expectations, what it was to be kind and confident, thoughtful, polite. Certainly, the guidance was meant to help me through life, to offer tools to navigate every sort of interaction and situation. Also, to express who I was and what I represented—my identity and place in the world.

Another lesson: On any occasion, you should always be prepared and able to contribute in one way or another. I was not precocious, but I was taught how to properly mix a cocktail. Tending to guests with a Tom Collins is a useful skill for a child to have. The hosts, my parents, wouldn't have to interrupt the flow of drinks or conversation. (Fill the glass with ice, use the first cube as a guide for how much alcohol to pour, mixer, stir, garnish.) As a child, I don't recall objecting to any of these teachings. They seemed reasonable, civilized, how a good person would behave and treat others. I accepted them all, uncritically.

In retrospect, I realize these life lessons were colored by my parents' mid-twentieth-century notions of what is proper, what is good, clean, and orderly.

Understanding what was "good" meant, naturally, that some things were "bad." Some things were to be avoided, were counter to our way of being (which was the correct way). I admit these particular prejudices—what was *bad*—I accepted as full truth. And here I'm going to confront one of those prejudices. I recall my mother stating more than once, and absolutely: "The homes of people with cats smell." Also, to me: "You would never want a cat." I'd never expressed to my parents a desire to have a cat, but somehow among the many ways we defined and presented ourselves, the distinction of being "dog people" rather than "cat people" was one to note. Should the question ever arise, I could blithely identify as a dog person since there was nothing at stake for me.

Along the way and as an adult, I'd visited the homes of friends who had a cat, or multiple cats, even dogs and cats. The cats as a whole seemed as indifferent to me as I was to them. I didn't dislike them; they were simply benign presences. They might walk across your lap if they felt like it, but they didn't require any attention. Dogs liked to be petted. Cats, it seemed to me, did not.

When I met my partner, A., he didn't have any pets. (I had a tiny frog and a couple finches. Which, as I write this, suddenly seems telling. Of what, I don't know.) With A., the dog person/cat person conversation didn't happen until we'd decided to move in together. We'd been together while keeping our own spaces in the East Village of Manhattan for quite a few years. But this was real moving in together, getting a place of our own to share.

As it turned out, A. is a cat person. He had always had a cat. Growing up, his family had numerous cats that came and went following their whim or hunger. Almost immediately upon moving into our new (very old) home, A. expressed his desire to adopt one. This was a wrinkle I hadn't expected. I knew I didn't want a smelly home, so I managed to avoid the issue deftly for several years, calling upon the dangerous and dust-producing renovations we were taking on. The conditions would be unhealthy for a pet, and it was a solid argument. However, we eventually got things in relatively good order, and a cat seemed perfectly feasible. Also, the issue of odor wasn't confirmed by anyone I knew with cats, so beyond a very faint, lingering filial duty to honor a canine-over-feline affinity—which I'd eventually confront with my parents—I didn't have particular objections. So sure, let's get a cat.

We started at Liberty Humane Society in Jersey City where we'd moved. A. had an idea of the type of cat he wanted (he insists some cats can have a green cast to their coats, and that's what we were looking for), while my only request was that we adopt a kitten. I figured any potential neurotic behavior should be a result of living with us, not someone else. Right off, I liked a friendly black-and-white cat we met there, but since this was to be A.'s cat, I wanted to be sure we found exactly the cat he was looking for: a green cat, whatever that meant. We didn't have luck in Jersey City, so we crossed back over the river and learned that kitten season starts more or less in the spring. We'd made looking for a cat a regular weekend activity. I believe we'd started in the winter, not ideal. We set about visiting shelters, all virtually empty, filling out lengthy forms along the way. We started downtown and proceeded up. Finally, one weekend, we'd reached Animal Care and Control at 110th Street to be told yet again there were no kittens. While we were there, we decided to nose around. There was a family scouting for a kitten too, and as a group we went into rooms with stacked cages that felt a bit off-limits, but no one was around to object.

Sure enough, in an otherwise empty room of cages, one was filled with a pile of sleeping kittens. The moment A. and I looked into the cage, the kitten laying on top lifted his head, looked at us, and meowed, and we instantly agreed he was the guy for us. The family poking around beside us adopted too. These brothers all quickly found homes. I can't truly and honestly say our tabby kitten had a greenish cast to his coat, but in certain light we thought maybe. After very lengthy debate, we named the kitten

Coven (long o: ko-vhen, a reference to the documentary *American Movie*).

Since bringing Coven home, I can't imagine living without a cat. Coven activated our home, made it alive. He was very beautiful even though he's supposedly a common sort. People found him remarkable. I can't say why exactly, but it was true. He would inspire comments on his appeal while simply laying down doing nothing.

The first night we brought Coven home, I worried about him not having the comfort of another heartbeat to sleep with. So, I slept on the bathroom floor with him nestled next to me. A. was an old hand with cats and had no worries, but I was new to this. Coven was very tiny and had such big ears. His markings were elegant and symmetrical. I sang songs to Coven constantly, in all of which he was the subject. I talked to him; he'd talk too. It delighted me when I'd be upstairs and call his name and he'd poke his head through the banisters to look at me, then pad up to keep me company. I called Coven the best little kitty in the world, and for me he was. Often, when I'd work, he'd be on the corner of my drafting table with his head under the warmth of the lamp. I felt both of us content.

The human–animal bond—and more specifically, why living with a cat is satisfying—has certainly been studied, the benefits to our well-being measured and cataloged. I'm confident these studies exist, although I haven't read any. I don't have thoughtful insight into the scientific aspect of keeping pets. For me, what I experienced was, I suppose, a kind of first love. Coven belonged to A., but we had our own special bond.

Coven was plagued with some health issues that worried us initially, but we managed. While the general consensus remains that online medical advice is less reliable than a doctor visit, we found it otherwise. Coven had some urinary issues that the vet suggested required exploratory surgery, "to be sure, and rule some things out." This seemed creepily opportunistic and sounded like an upsell in treatment designed to take advantage of our attachment. Our online research consistently tied Coven's symptoms to being a neutered male. A special diet was recommended, and it turned out to be an effective treatment. We never returned to that vet.

There were other persistent things, like ear mites, but we treated them. He got worms once too, which was a super disgusting discovery. We think he may have gotten them from eating a mouse. One morning, Coven was in my studio, sitting very erect. I said, "Good morning" and he didn't respond, just sat there not moving a muscle. It was strange. I said, "Hey Coven, what's up?" and he didn't move from his spot in the middle of the floor. I got close to him and noticed at his feet a little dead mouse, most of one anyway. Of course, I can't be sure, but I think he was really proud of catching the mouse and was waiting to show me. You may find it ghoulish, but I was indeed very proud and gave him many congratulations.

I've been writing in the past tense, so I'm sure you understand Coven is gone now. My very dear and daily companion lived what I've been told was a good, long life. Thinking of him now, I'm already finding it difficult to type and see the computer screen. Coven was the best little kitty in the world. I loved him very much. And I miss him. I thank you for indulging me in sharing a bit about him. I still have the xeroxed page from when he was first brought to Animal Care & Control of New York City. The printout has a little picture of tiny Coven in the upper left-hand corner. They gave it to us, along with other documents, when we collected him for the journey from 110th Street in Manhattan to 5th Street in Jersey City. The page details—Name: UNKNOWN, Color: BR TIGER & BR TIGER, Breed: DOMESTIC SH, Sex: MALE, Markings: FOUR KITTENS IN A BOX, Found at: FD IN BOX 1553 STARLING AVE. I sometimes think about visiting Starling Ave. I don't know where that is, but maybe someday.

When Coven came into our lives, I knew I'd eventually want to warn my parents of his residency. From them, I was anticipating resigned disappointment. They would manage to communicate their disapproval with veiled politeness. Perhaps they'd start to pause before sitting down anywhere, stealthily examining cushions for the abundance of cat hair that was sure to cover every surface of my home. Scented candles would suddenly become the gift of choice to bring with each visit. I've brought them what I knew would be disappointing news before (I dented the car! I'm a fine arts major! I bought a fixer-upper!), so I proceeded with the announcement, prepared to endure the displeasure of these avowed dog people. When I shared that a little kitten was now part of my family, their eyes brightened. They were absolutely delighted. I thought, *Really? But we're dog people. You told me as much.* They just smiled and immediately shared the names of each of their own kittens they'd had as children. Wait. What?! You had cats? And the names! Snowball for my mom, and Mittens for my dad (it may have been the other way around), but really?! My incredulity at the fact that my parents had lied to me about cats for all these years was met with what I should have learned from past, similar experiences. There wouldn't be an explanation, or an apology, or denial, or anything other than the two of them sharing a sort of conspiratorial laugh and a very particular facial expression which in this case communicated: How in the world would anyone not want an adorable little kitty? Then: Why are you always so tense? You're making something of nothing. And finally: Coven, what an unusual name, so fun. Raymond, you should relax more, why don't you go ahead and make us all cocktails.

One last note: The cat currently in residence at our house is named Juan Gris, named for his gray coat and after the Spanish Cubist painter. He has button eyes and is very adorable. He jumps on our heads to wake us every morning and likes attention. Also, if a person who keeps a cat has a home that smells, it is the person's fault, not the cat's.

THE Top 10 Reasons #NOVARULES

BY: NICOLE² @ SOUTH STREET ARTMART

10. Fashion Forward.

May 8, 2016

9. Ride or die BFF.

September 29, 2015

5 YEARS AGO

timehop

=D

8. SUPER Helpful.

7. Knows her worth.

6. Life of the party.

5. Knows her angles.

February 24, 2014

4. Looks great in gym shorts.

May 26

3. Will not be denied

August 23, 2013

2. Excellent @ cosplay.

LUCKY AND ANIMAL

Tuan Vu Tran

LUCKY IS SO LUCKY

I met Lucky when she was only a tiny baby at the shelter. It wasn't kitten season, so the only two kittens available for adoption were her and her sister, Animal. Lucky was on her back sleeping peacefully. She was such a pretty cat, so it was no surprise that everyone wanted her. A raffle was to be held to see who could adopt her, and I won. I'd never won anything in my life, but looking back now, I feel like I hit the jackpot. We were so lucky to have found each other, and this is why I named her Lucky.

LUCKY IS SO THOUGHTFUL

Lucky can sense when I'm stressed out or feeling down. It's a complete mystery how she knows, but she comes right up to me and meows like crazy. She then licks my arm, flops her whole body down right next to me and lays there purring loudly. She must know what she's doing because it makes me feel better everytime.

LUCKY IS SO TALKATIVE

Lucky is always talking. If I'm on the phone, she runs up to me and meows non-stop, just trying to be a part of the conversation. This is especially amusing when I'm trying to talk to someone on the phone because it always makes them laugh on the other end. Lucky also loves to sing. She will frequently sing very loudly while looking at herself in front of the mirror.

LUCKY+ANIMAL BOOKMARKS

✂ Turn over and carefully cut-out along dotted lines on the back

THE LOVABLE LUCKY

[GET TO KNOW HER WITH THIS BOOKMARK]

Lucky is a female Calico cat and her sister is Animal. She's a very picky eater, so she won't eat most things unless it's one of her favorites. Lucky's hobbies include sleeping, eating, playing and then more sleeping. Lucky is a scaredy-cat. She is especially scared of barking dogs. Lucky likes to sleep everywhere, depending on her mood. She will sometimes sleep on the bed, under the bed, on the desk, on the cat tree, in a pet cube, inside of an empty cardboard box, in the cupboard, at the top of the stairs, or curled up next to her owner. Lucky will always come running as soon as her owner calls out to her. Lucky is a very loyal cat.

THE ADORABLE ANIMAL

[GET TO KNOW HER WITH THIS BOOKMARK]

Animal is a female Tortoiseshell cat and her sister is Lucky. Her name's supposed to be "Anne" for short, but she only responds to "Animal". She's not a very picky eater, so she'll pretty much eat everything. Animal's hobbies include sleeping, eating, playing and then more sleeping. Animal is fearless and not many things will scare her. She likes to sleep under the bed covers. Animal will groom herself thoroughly, then burrow under the bedsheets. She will settle in the center of the bed for a long nap. Once asleep, she won't wake up for anything. However, with food always on the mind, Animal will come running if she hears a bag of cat treats being shaken.

✂ Carefully cut-out along dotted lines

LUCKY+ANIMAL'S TIC-CAT-TOE

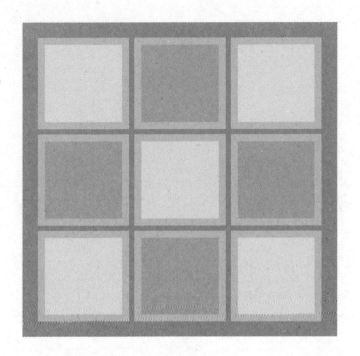

INSTRUCTIONS ON HOW TO PLAY

For two players. One player is **LUCKY**. The other player is **ANIMAL**. LUCKY will go first. For the games that follow, take turns. Each turn, place a token in one of the nine grid sections. Three in a row of one symbol wins. It's a draw if the grid is filled but no one has three in a row. If a draw, clear off all pieces from the board and start a new game.

✄ Turn over and carefully cut-out along dotted lines on the back

LUCKY+ANIMAL'S TIC-CAT-TOE

Back

LUCKY · LUCKY · LUCKY · LUCKY · LUCKY

ANIMAL · ANIMAL · ANIMAL · ANIMAL · ANIMAL

THANKS FOR PLAYING!

I hope you liked playing with **Lucky + Animal** right meow. It's been lots of fun.

TOEKNEE TUAN VU TRAN · **STUDIOKNEE**TOE

✂ Carefully cut-out along dotted lines

ANIMAL'S MINI STORIES

ANIMAL IS SO WILD

I met Animal when she was only a tiny baby at the shelter. It wasn't kitten season, so the only two kittens available for adoption were her and her sister, Lucky. She was talking to me like crazy, so I made her my first choice. She was so cute but wild looking, so the others overlooked her and wanted to get Lucky instead. However, they began asking about Animal once Lucky was claimed. The worker told them, "Sorry. He's already picked her when no one else wanted her." I have fond memories of that day. I picked her first, and in return, she's rewarded me with her gratitude and affection.

ANIMAL IS SO INDEPENDENT

Animal has always been a loner. She likes to perch on top of the cat tree so she can stare at everyone going by. Though she mostly keeps to herself, Animal will still come by regularly to say meow in her own way. Every night when I lay down for bed, she runs up to me, climbs onto my chest while purring and kisses me on the chin. She does this to say goodnight, and then she's off again to explore the house.

ANIMAL IS SO ADORABLE

I picked Animal because of how talkative she was at the shelter. She loves to talk, and she could go on for hours. She has the ugliest yowl that I've ever heard, but it's so adorable in its strangeness. I like that she talks to me so much, but sometimes I wish I knew what she was saying.

ACCIDENTAL RESCUES

Leah McNaughton Lederman

Charlie stood here in the yard just last week, talking about his plans for the pole barn, idly picking up each kitten that walked by, laughing when they wriggled in his callused hands.

"Look at that fat little belly!" the big man cooed.

"Put her down, Charlie!" Janine had fussed at him. She'd smoothed each kitten's ruffled fur before it bounded away, colliding with one sibling or another.

Little Lugnut didn't mind Charlie one bit. She'd prowl through the tall grass when she saw him, then plop at his feet. She was the biggest and the slowest of the litter, and she and Charlie loved each other.

Like most kittens, these were an accident. Our roommate at the time, convinced she'd found our missing tabby, corralled this cat into the little shed attached to the garage. She called me at work to announce she'd found Izzy—"and she's pregnant!"

That night, the cat unleashed six kittens into our lives. And she was definitely not Izzy. Mamacat was a sweet honey-mustard-colored thing with inquisitive golden eyes. She seemed content to stay in our shed, kneading her claws into her favorite imaginary pillow.

Once they'd moved past the larval stage, the kittens spread into the yard, sharing gambols and choreographing *Matrix* stunts. Occasionally, they'd stalk me or swat at the pages of my book. They loved me because I fed them. Each night after work, I'd visit and sprinkle food into the row of mismatched plastic bowls. They'd erupt into a raucous chorus of mews and purrs when they saw my flashlight, hopping over each other at their makeshift trough.

I was in the shed the day it happened, nuzzling into the little gray one's fur, inhaling its musky kitten scent. Josh came in with a face like granite and sat down. I did not want to hear what he was saying. They were the wrong words; he must have gotten them mixed up.

There had been an accident. It was messy. Charlie, his stepfather, was dead.

Josh waved the string of his hoodie at the orange tabby, who crawled into his lap to gnaw on it. The kitten broke out into a gravelly purr and Josh smiled. It was like someone had opened a curtain in a dark room.

"She's got her motorboat going," I said.

"Sounds like her vocal cords are on training wheels." I laughed but Josh didn't. The smile fell from his face and his chin fell to his chest, vmuffling his words. "What am I going to do?"

The steaks Josh cooked were perfect, but the dinner was hard. Sitting there with his mother, our words tripped in their hurry to get to the punchline; our laughter hit a higher, strained pitch. Anything to keep the silence from settling in.

The funeral had been the day before. Janine hadn't wept for the shock of it all. Charlie's death had coiled around our necks, binding us together and isolating each of us at the same time. We'd insisted Janine have dinner with us, if only to stave off the solitude ahead.

The conversation hit one of those empty silences and then we all heard it: a kitten calling for help. We hurried outside as one unit, Josh grabbing the flashlight from its place by the back door.

"It's coming from the garage," Janine said, huffing along.

She was right—when we entered, the meows were directly above, piercing, echoed by Mamacat, who paced the concrete floor, eyeing the hole-ridden ceiling.

"How did it get into the loft?" I asked.

Josh took one careful step at a time, aiming the flashlight where Mamacat directed him. "There." He wiggled the light on an exposed rafter, and a pair of round eyes reflected back. The huddled form stood up, meowing with what sounded like relief.

Lugnut. Of course it was Lugnut. She took a step forward, testing her weight, and poked her head down to look at us.

"The flashlight!" Panic hit me. "She'll come towards the flashlight!"

Josh was already charging forward, hopscotching over discarded tools and projects. He reached out his hand just as Lugnut lost her balance and toppled over the edge. She plummeted towards the floor, body flailing wildly with each moment the collision came nearer. Beside me, Janine pleaded "No, no, no" under her breath.

He caught Lugnut with one hand and pulled her into his chest, hunching his shoulders over her. There was a long, silent moment of collective disbelief. Finally, Josh uncurled and examined Lugnut, whose purr rattled from across the garage.

He looked over at us and grinned. "She's got about two pounds worth of cobwebs on her, but I think she'll be all right."

After we'd caught our breath and cheered a few more times, I reunited Mamacat and Lugnut and set them with the other babies to rest. Josh gathered scrap plywood and set about repairing whatever hole led to the rafters. Janine hadn't moved.

"Hey," I said, approaching her. "You want to go back inside? A glass of wine sounds nice."

She spoke to the floor with a trembling voice. "That could have been such a terrible, terrible accident." Above us, Josh paused in his work. She continued. "At least someone saved Lugnut. Why couldn't . . . there was no one there for my Charlie . . . I just wanted to hold his hand." Her lips crumpled, and she turned back towards the house, her shoulders so slumped she looked as though she might wilt back into the earth.

I caught up with her, and she let me guide her up the back steps. Inside, she sat on the couch, ignoring the glass of wine I'd poured for her. Josh had joined her on the couch when I came back from readying the guest bed, having insisted she stay.

She stared at the wall, her eyes glassy. "If it's all right," she said softly, getting up, "I think I'll turn in early."

Moments later, we heard the widow's muffled wail from behind the door.

PORTRAIT OF MOM

Melanie Rosato

THANK YOU LUCY AND SKETCH

Jay McQuirns

SKETCH

LUCY

THANK YOU LUCY AND SKETCH

BY JAY McQUIRNS

MARCH 2020

DOESN'T IT FEEL LIKE HE'S AROUND A LOT MORE THAN NORMAL?

IT'S HARD TO SAY. HE'S NOT REALLY MR. SOCIAL BUTTERFLY TO BEGIN WITH.

I DUNNO... SOMETHING'S DIFFERENT.

LET'S GO KNOCK OVER OUR WATER.

YAH!

LATER

WHY ISN'T HE CHASING US?

HE'S BEEN LOOKING OUT THE WINDOW FOR HOURS.

ESCAPE

Helen Kaucher

R amona has always been a wide-eyed, tumultuous goddess. Since our first meeting at the vet's office, I attributed her varied looks to a myriad of animals. She was an amalgamated creature composed of rabbit, screech owl, weasel, meerkat, panther, dragon, and pygmy marmoset—depending on her mood. There's no doubt her blood was too wild to be kept indoors.

I bought her a harness and leash to coax her on neighborhood walks, or to spend sunny afternoons basking in the grass. But even being on the porch terrified her, and, upon leaving the apartment, she would immediately slink towards the door to go back inside.

I tried to acclimate her to the harness for a few months, but to no avail. She would remain a windowsill cat.

In mid-March of 2020 I began a new stay-at-home discipline. After a week of vacillating between panic, calm, restlessness, and exhaustion, I decided to call the confinement an "Artist in Residence." It felt less foreboding than "quarantine," and held the suggestion that productivity and creativity were lurking between the walls.

My boyfriend Joey and I often joke that our apartment is actually "Ramona's Place." After all, she's there all day, every day while we pay her rent and utilities, scoop her poop, and serve her daily meals. It sounds like a pleasant life sentence compared to others, but I imagine such a wild nature stuffed inside her tiny body to be pure anguish.

When I started my new residency, I thought it only fair that we share the pronouncement of critical isolation.

Making creative plans started to get exciting, and I was thrilled I had the time to spruce everything up the way I've always wanted. Everything would be kept clean and organized. Each room would look just like every interior decorating catalog I've ever pored over, every cozy living room I'd visited, every studio space I'd seen utilized to its full, angular potential. We would relish in each sunlit room, living in ultimate, green-footed, patchouli-glazed harmony.

The washer and dryer in our building has never been operative since Joey moved in over three years ago. Due to the mechanical inconvenience (and the newfound, irrational fear of laundromats brought on by the pandemic), I began washing our clothes in the bathtub. Luckily, I am a task-minded human that lives by checklists and learning by action, so this potentially vexing development didn't disturb me. In fact, I began taking pride in my new peasant attitude and humble reliance on fair weather to dry our clothes. I fell in love with the way sunlight bleached our black clothing and how the air permeated the fibers with a sharp, feral wind. One evening, I mistakenly grabbed Ramona, who had nestled in a pile of black shirts that I was methodically scooping up to place in the laundry basket. Her little black body was perfectly curled up in our clothing, her glowing eyes widened by my mistake.

When, after a while, most of my panic-induced busy work around the house became exhausted, I started to germinate seeds in the bedroom windowsills. It's always been a dream of mine to have a fruitful garden plot, but because we rent, I stick to container gardening. One morning, while I was outside transplanting, the owner of the building pulled his utility van into the yard to have a poke around in the basement with the still useless washer and dryer. After some small talk, (which seemed to contain more lonely silence, unassuredness, and solidarity than ever before), he motioned to the planters near the stairs and said, "You know, you can have a bigger garden if you'd like."

Permission granted! The next day I dug out a six-by-four-foot plot near the staircase. Displacing the dirt was a minor deliberation, but I wound up dumping 120 gallons in the alley next to my neighbor's house. The newly packed dirt mound was a decidedly better neighborhood feature than plastic gin bottles and broken cinder blocks.

The garden was coming along splendidly. The only fracas present was the neighborhood gang of squirrels that swept through the yard to dig and bury peanuts in any area of loosened soil. Every planter and plot had to be covered with plastic or wire netting to keep them protected and contained.

Ramona and I spent most of every day together. I at my desk. She in the window next to me. If I was on the porch, she was on her hind legs peering at me through the screen door. When I tussled around in the garden, I could see her up in the kitchen window, a pair of floating eyes tilting back and forth like the bubble of air inside a spirit level. When we read on the couch in the evenings, Ramona was perched on the pillow near my head, making gentle cooing and sighing sounds while resting her paw on my shoulder.

Opting for cheery music to fill the day, I rediscovered a love of 10,000 Maniacs, Natalie Merchant, and Tracy Chapman. Many of the tracks reminded me of my childhood, as my mother had played those albums often. I felt the translucent white curtains of my old living room bellowing through my body; I felt aired out and breezed through, just like the shirts on our clothesline.

One evening, as I was cooking eggplant moussaka, I ran out to the porch herb garden to grab some basil leaves. As I opened the door to come inside, Ramona bolted out of the apartment in a fever dash—low and fast. I ran down the steps after her, twisting my ankle and fumbling down the rickety wooden stairs that had swollen in the afternoon heat. I pictured her squished in the road and my heart quickened. There was nowhere sweet enough for her to safely hide in our neighborhood. When I rounded the corner after her, I saw her crouched in a patch of grass, listening to motors whiz by on the main road. Joey ran outside to help corral her, and we managed to trap her in the alley where I had dumped the dirt from the garden. She seemed to have fled regretfully, an assumption I made when Joey told me he saw her peeing while sprinting for refuge. She scurried towards Joey, and he was able to grab her while she seized the bone of his forearm in her jaw. As he ran up the steps with her squished against his body, blood trickled onto the planks of our wooden staircase. We washed his arm and prepared for a trip to the hospital to have the bite examined. Before we left, I found Ramona under the dresser and cleaned the blood of her combatant from her forehead.

Masks adorned, we left the hospital and headed to the pharmacy with Joey's arm bandaged up dramatically in layers of gauze to cushion the four pin-sized puncture wounds underneath. "Wonder" by Natalie Merchant was playing throughout the pharmacy when we entered.

Over the next few days, I read up on ways to prevent future cat escapes, which the cat community calls "door dashing." Some of the tactics a cat owner may implement: the squirt bottle method, greeting and rewarding while distancing from problem zones, entertainment and distraction, hormone therapy, and physical barriers. I settled on entertainment and physical barriers.

Since I already had a surplus of garden netting to keep out the squirrels, I created a homespun child gate and affixed it to the door and wall using velcro. The new installation sectioned off a forbidden triangle of space, making "Ramona's Place" slightly smaller than before.

Near the end of May, Ramona started to sit near the new gate to smell the fresh air blowing in through the screen, testing her new boundaries. The plants started pushing through their barriers, and I fumbled around with netting so the buds wouldn't become strangulated, wondering how much confidence to put in weaves of plastic.

Ramona exemplified that however free our imaginations may be, there is always the desire to flee our physical space, to run in the open air and feel unrestrained or otherwise out of control. I love her more knowing that she still has a wild, undomesticated core. There's a newfound bond we share as we sit together— whether one of us is outside looking in, or inside looking out.

BUSTER AND HELLSCREAM

Erin Wu

adventures begin

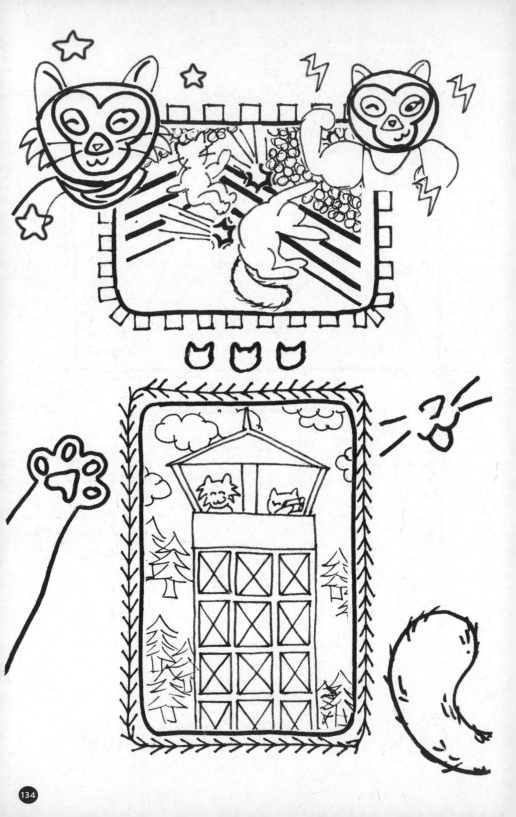

THE COLLECTIBLE CAT

Katie Haegele, illustrations by Caitlin Peck

KITTY PICNIC

One day a few winters ago, my partner Joe and I set up a stall to sell secondhand stuff at an outdoor holiday market, a sweet event at an urban farm on a rambly old property near us. They have a chicken coop and a beautiful old house with huge doors and stained glass windows, and they were selling Christmas trees and wreaths and hot cider.

We sell at markets like this sometimes. We so enjoy finding neat old things that we started reselling some of them in an effort to keep our scavenging habit from blossoming into a hoarding problem. It's fun, sitting there with our janky old stuff, talking to people about the Garfield jelly glasses and homemade lamps encrusted with seashells. On this particular day, though, there were a few inches of snow on the ground, and we were stuck standing in it, in the shade. I was wearing my snow boots, but my feet got too cold anyway and it was making me grouchy, so I left early to catch the bus home.

Once I'd walked the few blocks to the bus stop, I started to get that feeling I almost always get when I go for a walk by myself, that I could go on walking forever—a feeling of coming back to life. I decided not to bother with the bus. I knew I could walk the whole three miles to my house taking just two streets, a fact I found pleasing enough to make it worthwhile. The day was bright, and I looked at everything. For a while, the neighborhood was all stone walls wrapped in winter vines and Victorian mansions, some of them restored to the glory of their youth, others blank-eyed and haunted with rotting porches and sagging roofs. This vibe eventually gave way to a mile or so of a harder urban area, where the buildings were less leisurely, crowding in next to each other and muscling right up to the sidewalk. I walked past corner bars with signs that hadn't been changed since the '60s and beauty supply shops that were closed on a Sunday. There was one old store, in a building made of red-painted brick, that looked no different from the others except that, as I walked by, a young man carrying a car seat with a very little baby in it pushed the door open, and the sound of a whole church's worth of people singing hymns burst out the open door for one loud, bright moment. I don't know if storefront churches are a thing in other cities, but we have a lot of them in Philly. It's magical, the way these spaces have been reimagined and given new life. The guy and I startled smiles out of each other as I passed, and then the door fell closed behind him and the street was quiet again.

My stupid snow boots are half a size too small, and, by the time I got to my house, both of my big toes were numb, but there was a package wrapped in kraft paper stuck in my door. It was addressed to me from my friend Melba—some kind of surprise, a Christmas gift, I guessed. Seeing it there made me feel smart and correct for choosing to leave the event early and come back home, where I could savor the feeling of opening the gift alone, as I was meant to, which would cancel out the feeling of being foolish for walking all that way in bad shoes.

The package had a letter in it and *two* Christmas presents, both cat-themed: a cat purse and a cat puzzle. The purse is one of those tapestry ones with a woven image of lots of cat faces in it—I know you know the kind I mean. The puzzle is an illustration of dozens of cats, all wearing clothes and acting like people, in a big outdoor summer scene called Kitty Picnic. Kitty Picnic is wonderful to behold. The cats in the picture are depicting early Americana with their style of dress and activity. There are "men" and "women" and "children" cats wearing straw hats, bloomers, and collared shirts and ties. They are playing baseball and sitting under parasols. They have cakes, hot dogs, and a pitcher of lemonade on their table, which is covered with a white tablecloth. It's almost hard to spot them all, but, looking at it now, I count 46 cats—on the playing field, around the table, on a wicker bench, and, in the most authentically cat-like poses, hiding in a tree and playing with a skunk.

I smiled as I looked at Kitty Picnic, but understood sadly that I would never be able to do it. I haven't done a jigsaw puzzle since I was very little, I would guess, since I have no memory of ever having done one. My only association with them is a feeling of refusal, like: *No, I don't like puzzles*, or, *No, I'm not good at that.* It's probably because my sister *was* good at puzzles, and, if you have only one same-sex sibling, then you know that both people seem to exist merely to highlight some difference in the other. Liz liked puzzles, so I couldn't. Why bother? She was so good at doing puzzles, in fact, that she would quickly finish one and then want to do it again right away, so my mother would turn the pieces upside down to make it more interesting for her. *La-di-frickin'-da.* I hung the cat purse over my desk chair where I could enjoy looking at it until I got a chance to use it, and I stashed Kitty Picnic in our spare room where I *wouldn't* have to look at it, since all it would do was make me feel glum.

A few weeks after this, I threw a birthday party for Joe, and our friend Julia came. Julia is a warm, mellow woman who laughs easily and is a great party guest. She's a good talker and is always happy to meet our other friends. She also once attended a birthday party for our *cat*, which should give you an indication of just how nice she is. Before she left to go home that evening, I told her we should get together one day soon for coffee or a beer.

"Well, do you like . . . puzzling?" she said around a laugh, in her agreeable way.

I took a moment to answer her as I thought about what she might mean. (I puzzled over it, if you will.) Then the image of the Kitty Picnic popped into my head.

"You mean like jigsaw puzzles?" I asked, wary but excited.

She did mean jigsaw puzzles. Her grandparents always have one in progress, she said, so working on them reminds her of family and, in particular, of Christmas, when they would all go to her grandparents' house and have cozy nights in. I had to admit, it sounded pretty nice.

So that's how I spent my Christmas holidays this year: watching that ridiculous cat picture take shape while Julia and I sat around the table and talked. We talked about TV shows and our families, plastic surgery and the royal family. I baked cookies before she arrived and made a little event out of it, put on the kettle for tea. It was a nice way to spend time with her. Before we started working on the puzzle I told her I was embarrassed by how bad I would probably be at it, but it turns out jigsaw puzzles aren't very hard to do after all, or at least this one wasn't; in fact, they are very satisfying to complete. When I finished the shrub with pink flowers, and when I found the last piece to the scene of a cat riding a tricycle that's pulling a red wagon full of smaller cats behind him, I felt a sense of mastery.

During one of our puzzle afternoons, though, I kept yawning.

"Boy, I'm sorry, I don't know why I feel so tired today," I said.

"It could be the puzzle," Julia said, nodding thoughtfully, and I think she was right. It had a meditative quality, putting the pieces together. I felt close to Julia as we chatted or worked in friendly silence, and to my friend Melba, too, the giver of the puzzle. I was keen to finish it and show her. It took us three sessions to complete, and a few days later, when the sun was out, I opened the curtains all the way and took a nice photo of it to email her. Then, like a Japanese movie monster, I destroyed the kitties' tiny civilization. I scrunched it up in my giant hands, making sure every piece came away from its clingy neighbor. I felt a little sad as I did this, but puzzles are not meant to be kept intact. I know some people do this—they Mod Podge their completed puzzles and frame them to hang on their walls. (I once had a neighbor who did this regularly and kept giving them to me, expecting for some reason that I would want to fill my apartment with these monuments to her sleepless nights.) But keeping the puzzle stuck together forever seems weird to me. I mean, as long as the thing still has all its pieces, it might be nice for someone else to enjoy doing it.

I won't sell the puzzle in our secondhand shop, though. The thrift store should have it. I put the pieces back in the box and mixed them around with my fingers, imagining the pleasure of anticipation that some future person would feel as they dumped them out onto their own table and got to work.

KRON TV LAMP

Whenever I watch a show or movie that's set in Los Angeles, my eyes just drink in the light that fills the cheerful rooms of the little bungalows everyone there seems to live in. White walls, bare floors, a colorful rug, a spiky plant, all of it brightened and washed in that pure yellow light.

The Netflix show *Love* takes place in L.A., with a bombshell character named Mickey, played by Gillian Jacobs. Mickey is a pretty specific kind of bombshell, a beautiful thirtysomething woman who, with her trendy clothes and sweet single-person's home, is still working the beautiful girl angle. I love the show for the realness of the characters and the way they talk and dress. Their rooms, too, look like places where real people live. In Mickey's pretty bedroom, she has a corner bookshelf that's awash with girly clutter, like the tide came in and left these treasures behind. Mickey is cool and tough, a complicated and unhappy person, but in her bedroom she's still a teenage girl, unembarrassed to like feminine things. This feels very familiar to me, very true. During one viewing of the show, I eyed the yellow shelf in the corner, loving all the details I saw there, and then I spotted it, a shiny ceramic statue of two Siamese cats. It looked like a mother cat with her baby tucked up close against her, and all four of the eyes were glowing with a strange red light.

The cat lamp!

I raised my eyes two feet above the TV to the shelf on our wall, where the identical cat lamp sat. It's a good two feet tall, and the cats' eyes are small almond-shaped holes, sliced out of the ceramic as cleanly as if with a cookie cutter. They're chocolate point cats, like our Siamese cat, Coco. They have creamy chests and bellies with dark brown feet, faces, tails, and ears. The cut-out eyes are supposed to shine with the light from a bulb inside the lamp, but unlike the one on the show, ours wasn't lit because we'd removed the electric element and were using the cats as a decorative figurine rather than a lamp.

We'd thought that's all it was at first—a statue. Joe and I spotted it at the same time, drawn to it as if by a magnet as we walked through the automatic doors at Savers, a huge thrift store in a strip mall that we love. We went to it wordlessly, in step with each other. Surrounding it on the shelf were its fellow figurines, many of them also ceramic and shaped like animals, but the Siamese cats were superior to the others. Bigger, more detailed, more unusual. I picked the statue up and saw that it had a cord dangling from the bottom. *Oh holy moly, it's a lamp!*

In point of fact, it is a *TV lamp*. I spent a good few hours learning about TV lamps from articles on the internet, the exhaustive website TVLamps.net being my primary source. By googling a description of my lamp and the company name printed on the bottom—Kron—I found the website and fell right down a rabbit hole.

When television was new, an article on the website reminded me, TV sets were a new kind of furniture in American households. The sets were most often large, self-contained pieces of wooden furniture that stood a few feet high, and people began placing these decorative lamps on top of them. The lamps were initially manufactured because everyone thought that watching a TV screen in a darkened room would damage their vision, but they soon became popular as decorations. Another article I read on TVLamps.net was titled "Tacky Treasures," a slur I take some issue with, but I guess I don't entirely disagree. The writer said that the most popular TV lamp motifs included wild animals like panthers, stagecoaches and wagon wheels, nautical stuff, and Siamese cats. In fact, TVlamps.net has a whole page dedicated to Siamese cat lamps. It was a popular image at the time, and there were dozens of different designs.

Though these lamps aren't rare, antiques dealers seem to be getting anywhere from thirty to four hundred dollars for them now. Joe and I paid eight dollars for ours and will never part with it. We think it's gorgeous, and the idea of TV art is touching to me. I like that we somehow intuited that the thing was made to sit on top of a TV and put ours on a shelf just above it, and I like that we later saw the lamp *on* TV. It's nice when things come full circle like that.

CROSS STITCH, 1657

I've been drawn to the idea of magic since I was a kid, like so many kids are, especially girls, I think. When I was older and read about the history of witchcraft in the West, I learned that being a "witch" in medieval Europe usually meant you were a woman who was weird in some way—you lived by yourself, maybe, or were childless, or you were a healer, or could read and maybe write. All of this information felt pertinent to me, a childfree, interestingly gendered book nerd. I got another thrill many years later when I understood that I could learn about herb plants and their uses, both practical *and* magical. That I could be a witch in my own backyard and kitchen, and it would only mean good things. Mysterious and darkly feminine and good.

To me, magic is about intention, energy, colors, history, the ancestors, the ocean, intuition, wisdom. I can gather together all the things I love the most, and they start to take this shape. Cats, plants, other women and girls, dancing, the moon, rainy days, the seasons and the way they change, music and books, and the act of writing itself—the way, when it's working right, you seem to step into the river of life that flows through everything all the time, and feel it flow through you.

A certain kind of woo-woo witchiness is talked about widely these days. In some circles, at least, it's safe and socially acceptable to say you're a witch, and it's fashionable to look like one, with long pointed nails and purple hair. I know a real spiritual practice isn't all about accessories, but it is a *bit* about that. The tools help you practice the rituals, and the aesthetic puts you in the right frame of mind. I like that I can move around my house and pass a handful of crystals on the kitchen table, an aloe plant by the sink, a row of essential oils in the medicine chest. These things remind me of the kind of woman I want to be, who I like to think I am.

To this end, I have a cross-stitched picture hanging on my wall that I made a few years ago, probably in the autumn, when I was feeling especially witchy. I worked the pattern, which is made to look like an old-fashioned sampler, in the colors it called for: black, orange, gold, gray, and brown. Halloween colors.

Traditionally, a sampler has an alphabet and the year it was completed. This one has both, and though it's a modern design, the year is 1657, a reference to those times when it was dangerous to be a witch, I guess. Some of the letters of the alphabet are replaced by small images. There's a moon for the letter *M*, an owl for *O*, a witch's pointed shoe for *S*, and of course, where the letter *C* should be, there's a cat. The cat is gray, not black, which I think is a nice touch, and though its back is arched, its tail is curled cutely so you know it's friendly.

Cats have long been thought of as witches' evil minions, which is stupid, but they are indeed magical. My cat Coco is pudgy and old, but she still manages to find new places in our house to hide and make me think she's actually disappeared. She is both her comical self and the mysterious spirit of the house, a little flame burning bright.

TWO NILLA COMICS

Missy Kulik

I have to brush the cat. She pretends not to like it, but secretly she does.

purr

purr

look at all this fur I brushed off of Nilla.

You should toss that fur outside for birds to use in their nest.

I think I will. That's called "up cycling."

each time I
make broccoli,
Nilla knows.

She sits behind
me and waits.
Sometimes she
paws at me.

Then I hand
her the stalk
of broccoli. She
sniffs it...

sniff
sniff

And she likes
to chew on
it!

MOVING THROUGH PIPPA'S MIND

M.J. Fine

February 11

*T*he day started totally normally—napping next to Lady in bed for eight hours or so, followed by a bit of anxiety when she took a shower, and then a cozy nine-hour snuggle session in the other bed while Lady worked on her laptop. Of course, midway through, I had to howl at her for a while to remind her that I could die if she doesn't feed me, and then I had to mewl a bit to let her know just how amazing the food was, and then I had to yowl at her to let her know where I yacked it up. Nothing out of the ordinary.

But then a weird thing happened. Sometime between my siesta and TV time on the loveseat, Mister brought in boxes. Not litter boxes, not scratchy boxes, and not little forts like the ones I used to squabble over with my ex, but big cardboard boxes. And not just one or two, like when my people get packages delivered, but enough boxes to shut out half the living room. I kind of remember that there have been times when there were too many boxes at once and the furniture disappeared, but that was eons ago. I was so young then, less than half the age I am now, and I was so all-consumed by my relationship that I don't remember how I felt about it. I'm not sure how I feel about it now, either, but I'm going to keep an eye on things.

February 18

There's not too much to report. The empty boxes seem to just sit there, piled high enough to block the window, but I haven't been motivated to sit there much lately anyway—not since my bird friend suddenly stopped coming by one day and I realized just how barren the stucco wall was without her. The days pass by in much the same way as always: Nap. Snuggle. Lunch. Siesta. Family time curled up in front of the TV. Dinner. It's been cold, so I stay as close to Lady as I can, but I'm also anxious enough that I've torn through two scratch boxes in the past couple weeks.

February 25

Something's happening, but I'm not sure what. Books started disappearing, then clothes, now art. Mister peels things off the wall and puts them in boxes, then Lady tapes the boxes and writes on them. She seems just as anxious as when she uses her laptop, but in a different way. Whatever they're doing, their anxiety makes them hold me tighter. I don't mind, but I wonder if they know they could scratch some of those cardboard boxes to let go of some of that anxiety. That always works for me.

March 4

I don't like where this is heading. Strange people keep coming to our apartment. They dart around the cardboard boxes that cover every surface, look out the window at the stucco wall, laugh at the two toilets near my litter box, and leave just as quickly. At least Lady is here all the time to whisper to me. It's not reassuring, per se, but I can tell she's trying. Probably trying to reassure herself as much as anything, though.

March 11

The nap bed and the work bed and the loveseat are the only surfaces not covered by boxes. Good thing there's nowhere I'd rather be. Whatever is going on, the days start in the usual way: naptime followed by snuggling against the heat of Lady's laptop, with a quick break for lunch. But nights are very different. Instead of TV time, Lady and Mister seem to leave and come back, leave and come back, leave and come back. They take boxes whenever they go, but the piles never seem to get any shorter. In fact, every time they come back, they bring back empty boxes, and it's funny how the boxes never stay empty long enough for me to climb into. Not that I would actually do that—it's something my ex loved, and the last thing I need is a fort all my own, with no one to squabble over it with. But I worry that once everything is off the walls and there's nothing left to put in boxes, the furniture will disappear again.

March 18

I had the strangest experience this week. While I hid in the bathroom, I could hear a fleet of strangers noisily entering the apartment. When they cleared out, most of the boxes were gone, but the furniture was still there. I was simultaneously so relieved and so anxious that I clawed at the loveseat and then yacked under the bed. Lady and Mister were gone for a long time. I mean, not as long as naptime, but longer than my siesta, for sure. Not that I could sleep at all.

When they came back, Lady put me in a box—not a cardboard one or that horrible plastic one I sit in while having a horrible time waiting for the horrible vet, but a mesh one. I could feel Lady's lap beneath my paws, I could hear her whisper above the whoosh of the engine, and I could even kind of see Mister sitting next to us, but my anxiety was through the roof and there was nothing to scratch, no place to yack. The whole ride probably took less time than it takes for me to scarf up my dinner, but illogical thoughts raced through my brain: They were going to give me away. They were going to dump me in the woods. They were taking me to a different vet. At one point, I even thought they might be misguidedly attempting to reunite me with my ex, wherever he is, or my old bird friend and her flock, who were all certain to be mocking me for my mode of transportation, however involuntary it was.

But then Lady let me out of the mesh box into the biggest space I've ever gotten to explore in my life, and it was not at all what I'd imagined.

The furniture was all new—and the same soft gray as my own fur—and just like that, all my anxiety was gone. I didn't have to sink my claws into the sectional sofa or gobble up my food and find a spot to purge it. I didn't need to sniff around for my people's old books and any trace of my ex that might have clung to the pages. I didn't feel obligated to claim a windowsill and spy on the neighborhood birds and squirrels and children and rats; there'd be plenty of time for that in the months to come.

I just wanted to climb up and down the staircase all night— how had I lived so long without knowing about staircases?—and sink into one of the many blankets that Lady and Mister had so thoughtfully planted both upstairs and downstairs(!), blankets that smelled familiar but felt softer and cozier than I remembered.

And although I'd never dreamed of having a place like this—a place so large that my litter box was in a closet of its own and not sharing a room with two toilets—I knew I was home. And I knew that I would never again want to nap next to Lady in bed for eight straight hours when I could have a whole sectional sofa to myself.

TIME'S PRECIPICE

Justin Duerr

THE CRIME CATS

Ivan Dellinger

10 2022

10 2022

SCARLETT

Joe Carlough

One day, back when I was in grade school and my sister Stacey was in college, we were returning from a day of errands with our dad. He pulled into the driveway in his beloved van, a monstrous green family van that we called Prime Time as though that were its name and not just the make of the vehicle.

Prime Time had a soft beige interior and a small TV/VCR unit between the front seats, and the back seat folded down into a pretty sizable bed. Supposedly, my dad would enjoy his work lunches in the van, rolling down the window shades and watching old tapes of *Seinfeld* in there. A little oasis in a long day of tedious warehouse management. It also had the words "Prime Time" stenciled on the top of the windshield, words we used to annoy him by saying them as quickly as we could every time we approached the van.

"Prime Time!" Stacey would say.

"Primetime!" I'd counter.

"Primtim!"

"Primpt!"

And we'd go on until we were basically just shouting noises with *p* and *t* sounds.

On this particular day, we all got out of the van and froze, all three of us; we'd heard a mewing.

My dad and I were big animal people. He'd taught me all the tricks: finding nightcrawlers on a wet night to go fishing the next day; paralyzing frogs with a flashlight and scooping them up, just to admire them and feel their soft bellies before releasing them; overturning rocks and logs and pulling out snakes and newts and beetles and grubs. So when we heard the mew, we went into overdrive. There was a kitten somewhere.

Within seconds, my dad was on his belly, fishing around under Prime Time with his long, adult arms, and, before we knew, it he had pulled out the tiniest, dirtiest kitten I'd ever seen. It couldn't even open its eyes. He cupped it gently in his hands and whispered something about being glad he didn't drive over it, and we all went inside.

He made a little nest for the kitten, which Stacey decided was named Scarlett, in an old Rubbermaid bin with some towels along the bottom to keep it soft. We put the bin up in Stacey's room, one of the two rooms on the second floor of our house (my brother Tommy and I had the other), so that we could keep her safe and keep our dog, Sparky, away from her. (Sparky was a husky mutt, a big dog—he probably weighed around sixty pounds. He had one of those great, fluffy tails that curled upwards. My parents picked him out at a pound because he had spunk. The story goes that all the puppies of the litter were nursing except Sparky, who was the runt, so my parents watched as he grabbed one of the other puppies by the back legs and pulled it away from the mother to make room. The morning we brought him home, he immediately took to Stacey, who named him Sparkles. We all loved Sparky, and he loved us back, but he was poorly behaved and a little too quick to act.)

Later:

"Hey mom, we found a kitten."

"We're not keeping it."

"But it's so little, we have to look after it. It'll literally die if we don't keep it."

"We don't need a cat, we have a dog."

"We have a chance to do something right for this animal."

"Sparky will never allow it."

He didn't. A couple weeks later, Scarlett was a mobile, funny, fuzzy little ball of energy, still not that great at walking but keen on trying. I came home from school one day and heard my dad call down to me from upstairs:

"Hey Jughead, is that you?"

"Yeah!"

"C'mere, I need your help!"

I bound up the steps two at a time, a habit I still haven't broken, and walked into a pretty weird scene: My dad was on his knees, with the kitten cradled in the crook of one elbow. That hand held a baby's bottle of milk he'd bought at a vet's office. His other arm was up in front of him, crooked sideways, his forearm pressing hard into Sparky's chest. The dog had a mean look in his eyes, which reminded us both of the intense, longing gaze he directed at squirrels.

He only started snapping and growling when I tried to pull him back. My dad rolled onto his back and used his legs to push the dog toward the door as I pulled on his collar. I finally wrestled him out the door and shut it tight behind me.

"Sparky finally found us up here," my dad said, defeated. "Now he's going to sit outside that door all day, every day."

It only took Stacey a couple days to find a home for Scarlett. The cat went to live in her friend's apartment and was renamed Francie. A couple months later, I asked about Scarlett, and Stacey told me she was doing well, and growing up fast, and that she was pretty vocal and sweet. The next time I asked, she'd lost touch with that friend, and Scarlett, like an old pen pal that moves before you can rekindle your friendship, was gone from my life for good.

Jared Power

Prize Zucchini,
I love you.
I love you when you bite
my toes
because I'm not wearing any
socks and you hate that.
I love you when you scream
to go outside, although I am
never ever letting you back
out there in the city.
I love you when you bite
my hair and insist I wake
up to feed you at 7am.
I love you when you
sit next to me on your
special chair when I draw.
I love you, my Prize Zucchini.

42773

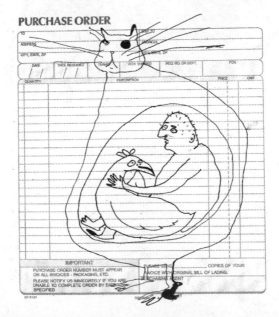

PURCHASE ORDER

FRANKIE, I MISS YOU

Marina Murayama

rainbowyama.bandcamp.com
murayama.bandcamp.com

I've got my head in the clouds again
I think I'm falling in love again
I know you're breaking my heart again
There's nothing I can do about it,

   nothing I can do about it...

Baby why'd you have to leave me?
You snuggle close and then you keep me
In the dark, I know–
Sometimes I get a little needy
But why do you have to tease me?

You hold me close then give cold
shoulders.
To think I thought that I'd had known you.
Sometimes I get a little needy
But why do you have to tease me?

With every rising moon and setting sun
Keep thinking what could've I done (to make you leave)?
With every setting sun and rising moon
I keep thinking, what can I do?

Frankie, I miss you
Mrs. Whiskers, I miss you
Fiona, I miss you
Fluffy... I miss you

MY BOY GEORGE

abby daleki

TW: death/suicide

When we first met, you fit in both my hands. Your first mom put a collar on you that she'd often forget to loosen as you grew. She kept you in a hamster cage at night because her mom wouldn't let you roam around. You were scared when we met and I could tell you hadn't had stability, but now you were My Boy George.

Actually, you'd gained two new moms—Mama D to start with, and now Mama B and me—and you weren't sure how to feel about that. Our three-bedroom duplex rental was a suitable home for you and a mediocre one for us humans. You didn't mind the fly infestations in my bedroom: more things to play with! With all of us going to school and working part-time jobs, you had a lot of time to yourself. I often wondered if you enjoyed the solitude or wished we were around more, but by the way you nipped at our feet and our ankles when we walked, I imagine you were just trying to get some attention. The unfinished basement where we kept your litter box (which we certainly weren't perfect at keeping clean) became a much larger litter box in the dirt under the steps. You liked to jump in the fridge when one mom opened the door, and a little bit later, I would open it again and you'd pop out. You loved to run away as soon as we opened the door to the house, and I would find you waiting to be let back in when I got home from work.

And then—something happened. You weren't sure exactly what was wrong, but you couldn't find Mama D. Her door was closed and you couldn't get in. I was gone, and Mama B came home from work. You were such a good boy and let her know that something wasn't right. She noticed you were acting strange and she investigated further. That was the night we lost her. That was the night everything changed.

Many days went by when Mama B and I would stop by to feed you and check on you. I'm so sorry we left you alone for so long. Mama B couldn't bear to see you because you reminded her of Mama D. So I swept in and you were mine. When I brought you to our friend Jenn's, the kitties there didn't like you. But we managed, didn't we? She was so compassionate to let us stay with her until we collected ourselves. After all, we were back together again—it was us against the world. Soon after, I was able to find a place for just us. Just you and me. My boy George, with his forever mom.

But there was still something missing. You were bored when I was off at work or school and you were pretty mad at me for that. Did you think getting you a little sister was a bad idea at first? I know you did. But you warmed up to her pretty quickly. The way you took her in like she was your baby. She loved her big brother and she still does. And you loved her, because you finally had someone to play with and chase after when mom was gone. You had someone to help you make bad decisions, like getting into a bag of chips or jumping into the sink to lick the dirty dishes. You were a team of two now. Then we moved cross-country, then a little further north. Then we moved back, and again and again and again. And then you gained *another* sister, and finally a dad—and boy do you love him. We're all pretty happy, aren't we? You get "your" chair, Mimi gets her bean bag, and Daisy gets the whole first floor. Life was pretty tough at first, and I regret it every single day. But I've always promised you one thing: you're the best boy in the whole world, My Boy George.

CATS IN TREES, STUDY #4

Nicholas Beckett

HAUNTED-HOUSE CAT

Vanessa Berry

Most of the neighborhoods around where I live have a few houses that are conspicuously run-down, in need of paint and repair, and surrounded by overgrown gardens. These houses are fascinating in the same way old photograph albums are, the kind you might find discarded, or for sale in an antique store. The people in the photographs inside such albums are strangers, but there's something familiar and captivating about them, the way their lives seem to be both like, and unlike, yours.

If you look closely as you pass by these houses, you'll most likely see cats hanging around. Cats are attracted to places where there are cracks and nooks and places to hide. They lie out amid the long grass of the gardens, or they lounge on the sun-warmed concrete of the front steps or the paths. If you stop and try to coax them over, mostly they just stare back at you, unmoved.

One particular house of this kind is on a corner and is square and painted white. It has a fence that's as irregular as a row of crooked teeth. People stare at it as they walk past, wondering who lives there, and sometimes they point out the black cat with a white chest and feet that sits out in front of it. Some people try to entice her over to them, but there's only one person who can get up close to her, the woman who lives in the house: me.

Every morning when I open the door, I look for her. Sometimes she's already there, sitting by the shoes and potted plants on the landing. Or if not, she soon appears from a gap in the foundations of the house, trailing cobwebs, blinking her way out of sleep. Good morning Soxy, I say, as she comes up close and pushes her head against my hand, then turns around and nudges me again, and again. Most days start like this, and the scene always feels like the beginning of a fairytale.

Soxy's domain is the earthy, spiderwebbed cavern under my house. Having the wariness of a cat that has never lived with people, she won't come inside, but whenever I go out she appears, as if she has the ability to materialize from thin air. We live our days alongside each other, but I can't claim her as mine in the way of a pet. Instead, I think of her as a companion spirit. During the day as I sit at my desk, she sleeps under the house, curled up in the corner underneath my room, or I can see her through the window, curled up against the fence.

She's a wise cat, a watcher, seeming to register everything that moves through or past the garden which is her domain. She shares it with another cat, her sister Seeka, who is her inverse, white with black patches. Seeka is a less enigmatic character, and round as a marshmallow from the ample feedings by the street's multiple cat ladies. She has little interest in me unless I'm holding a bag of Whiskas or the "party mix" treats I sometimes give to them. Soxy also has a taste for the party mix, but a lot of the time she is less interested in food than in observing me, as if I'm a puzzle she's continually trying to figure out.

Soxy and Seeka appeared as kittens during the year of the black-and-white street cats, when their numbers grew into the dozens. Then, to walk down the street at night was to run the gauntlet of their flashing eyes, and they would scatter as I approached, so it was as if the shadows were alive. Each had a feature to distinguish it from the others. One had a black patch over an eye, like a pirate. Another had a funny little head, disproportionately small. Another had black and white blotches like it was a miniature Friesian cow. At the peak of the street cat population explosion, one of the residents of the apartment building around which they were concentrated progressively rounded them up. She took them to the vet to be desexed before returning and releasing them. Now, seven years later, only a few of the cats from this time remain, those like Soxy and Seeka who have found positions of relative protection and have people looking out for them.

So, when people ask if I have a cat, I pause. I have Soxy, I reply.

Opening the front door, I see her. She's sitting at the foot of the steps, peering up at me as I look out towards the street. Cars are parked tightly all along it during this time in which everyone's staying at home, waiting out the pandemic lockdown. Another bus goes past, again empty of passengers. With few other sanctioned reasons to be outside, more people than usual are out walking. Almost all of them stare intensely at my house as they go by. But Soxy and I are in our own story, independent of all this. She has cobwebs on her ears from her nights spent in spidery dreamland. I am wearing the black quilted jacket that I've taken to now that I have been spending every day at home. It has deep pockets in which I keep tissues and pens and Post-it notes to catch ideas. I move to sit on the front step, and Soxy comes up by my side, and we linger here, haunting the house together.

KEEP SMILING!

What's the good of Crying over spilt Milk ? I don't!

CAT TAT

Yolie Contreras

Frida passed in December 2021. A week before Christmas. If you knew Frida, this checks out fully. She was notorious amongst our friends and family for being one of the meanest cats they've ever met. She would hiss and scratch everyone. Her hatred and displeasure did not discriminate.

Which is why whenever we did get some love kernels, it felt well-earned. Frida really did have her moments of pure love and sweetness. Times when she would begrudgingly let me hold her for a few minutes without growling. Or when she would kiss us right on the nose with a solitary lick. She would only do this with my husband and me, so it felt extra special knowing we were the only two people in the entire world that Frida would show affection to.

We lived this way for eleven years. Taking her with us through various moves from Tempe to Phoenix to Long Beach to Los Angeles and finally Tucson. It was never an option to leave Frida behind when we moved. We paid the extra rent and security deposits each time, knowing full well that she could care less and in no way had really earned this adoration. She was always there though: when my husband and I got our first place together, when we got married, when we bought a house. I honestly couldn't fathom a life without her and joked that she would outlive us or, at the very least, be with us well into our forties. (We were in our early twenties when we adopted her.)

She came from humble beginnings, being born under my friend's house in downtown Phoenix. I saw a photo of this small, flea-ridden furball and knew she belonged to us. From there, I brought her home, cleaned off her fleas and her swollen eye, and started a long journey with the meanest cat in the world. I think one of her saving graces was that she was so beautiful. White fur, gorgeous yellow eyes, and a pink nose made her irresistible.

How do you memorialize a cat who, at the same time made your life miserable, also made it full? Why, you get a tattoo of her, of course. I had gotten used to looking at her face for eleven years, and I needed to commemorate that. So now, on my right bicep, I have a cat tattoo, or a cat tat if you will, of Frida in all of her glory. You can even see her trademark crooked ear from when she somehow scratched the shit out of it and it remained forever bent.

I'm glad I brought her back to life in some way because her mean little attitude always meant we were home.

A MIRROR

Enx Eeden

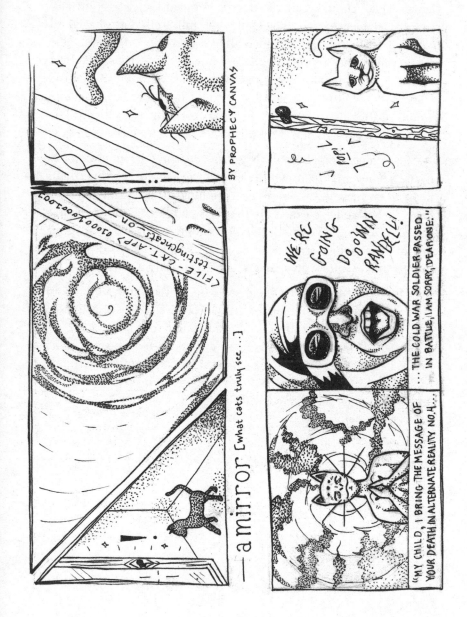

AMBASSADOR KITTY

Ailbhe Pascal

*F*uly, 2011: I was in Istanbul for the summer, and I was lost. I had just wrapped a month-long kitchen/farm/activist job, one that included housing and left me with a minor existential crisis in its wake. I was oozing *what-now?* energy in a cheap hostel. I wanted my whole life to be spent sitting by the sea with my girlfriend and my huntress cat, Fiona. Too bad my sweetie and my sweet familiar were back in the States. I wanted my Istanbullu friends to spend time with me, but they all were living their own lives with their own families. For a while, I slept off hot days and wrote through the night, but when I hit writer's block, the music of Florence Welch kept me company as I idled my time with fishermen on the Bosphorus.

It sounds idyllic, but my Turkish accent was bad and I was lonely. I looked up Mediterranean ferry passages and decided I would travel to the island of Lesvos, where I could recite Sappho's fragments on the rocky shores of her homeland. This, my fantasy queer rite of passage, gave me new purpose with my time in Istanbul. I had come out as pan only months earlier and, yes, I had baby dyke problems. I bought a Greek phrasebook and drew maps of the island.

Time came to get tickets, and my day started much the same as it had for the past week. I rolled out of my bunk, climbed up out of the cavernous basement where at least thirty people slept every night, went to the complimentary breakfast buffet (to stock my pockets with a days' worth of bread, cheese, and olives), and then I was out, baby! The sky was clear, the breeze was calm, and it was time to weave my way to the sea.

The next moment is frozen in my memory. I was lightheaded and couldn't hit all the notes in Florence's "Between Two Lungs." I stood in the shade, willing my voice up and down, confused about why I couldn't sing a song that was usually easy for me, when, *hello!*, here came sauntering a striped calico.

If you've been to Istanbul, read about the city, or even seen it on TV, you know: there are cats everywhere. There are thousands of them on the streets. This creature was a member of a colony that might outnumber the city's human population. But she introduced herself to me, and then, it seemed, sang with me. She mewed in tune, and when we were done, I had the energy to make it down the hill.

Street Kitty followed me, then led me, looking over her shoulder to make sure I followed. While I was intent on a paved, flower-lined route, she hooked right and took me down a broken-staired street covered in shadow, moving ever towards the sea. I stopped for a minute, and she paused with me, petting my legs and mewing. I photographed her with my polaroid, because I knew I had made a new friend. But reaching back in my bag, my arm throbbed. It looked bruised. *When did that happen?* I wondered, but Kitty was on the move.

We were moving faster, and suddenly the alley spilled out into a wide promenade where travelers like me could board ships large and small. I spotted the ticket booth for Greece-bound boats, turned back around, and Kitty was gone. The sun was now high and unforgiving, but I was going to embrace it and get my ticket . . .

Well, I don't remember fainting or how long I was out, but I awoke on the ground like from a dream. My "bruise" had taken on a malicious color, and it stung. I wasn't going to Lesvos after all.

Panicked, I asked for a hospital. For the first time, I didn't notice if people made faces at my accent. *Where is the nearest hospital?* I started my way back up the hill in the direction I was pointed in, and sure enough, Kitty was there waiting for me. If it weren't for the photo, I would have thought I made her up. She accompanied me step-by-step to the emergency room and waved her tail goodbye. It was so good, it had to be true.

After my spider bite (brown recluse!) mended, I hoped to meet my calico friend again. I was the stray in her city, and, in my summer of discontent, she had shown me excellent care. I bought a can of sardines and carried it with me for the rest of my time in Istanbul, in case I'd ever be given the opportunity to thank her. Her white boots never made their way into my life again, but still today, when I close my eyes and think of the word *magic*, I picture her staring up at me, inexplicably singing a British pop song.

THE CAT DAYS OF SUMMER

Alexis Campbell

I sometimes think that my cat is not meant to be my cat because he is much cooler than me.

I'm not just saying that. Augustus is the greeter at every open door. The attention whore at every gathering. The class clown. He talks to everyone (even that one guy who everyone knows hates being around *those types*, but then twenty minutes into the party is caught trying to nose-butt with the best of 'em, saying "But it's different with this one!"). Gus hasn't met a human he doesn't like, and he's been known to convert the staunchest of anti-catters.

So it's no surprise that in his youth, Gus had already made a reputation for himself. Back then, his name was Houdini. As in the escape artist. Because Gus had a habit of escaping Pet Farm, the outdoor pen of the summer camp where he had been taken at eight weeks old to teach children how to care for pets. I can't say I blame him for wanting to ditch the responsibilities that had been thrust upon him.

A few months earlier, in the existential dread of being one year away from graduating with an English degree, I applied for a summer camp counselor job on a whim. I was struggling with the whole idea of college and ruminating on the unfairness of getting a roommate my freshman year that peed on the carpet when she came back to the dorm room drunk. So naturally, in a depression-induced manic high, a moment between depressive episodes, I thought, "I'm taking control of my life," and "This will be the summer where I find myself and have a good time doing it, damn it!"

The six kittens brought in for the Pet Farm activity had everyone excited even before camp officially started. Three orange ones, a calico, and two tabbies, newly weaned from their mom. All the counselors threw around the term "barn cats" reverentially, like they were scrappy survivors of small-town farm life instead of a matter of overpopulation for the owner of the cat that got knocked up on their property and who subsequently placed an ad on Craigslist for the low, low price of OBO ("or best offer").

I asked one of the counselors who ran Pet Farm what would happen to the kittens after the summer ended.

"We sell them to anyone at camp who wants them for $25 each," she said.

"Is there a counselor discount?" I asked. Only partially joking. I wasn't making much at the summer camp, considering the hours and emotional turmoil I put into the job, and I pettily didn't want to give them $25 for a cat they just wanted to get rid of at the end of the session.

Apparently, the yearly promise of kittens was a huge draw for some kids to enroll in camp, and a portion of those kids managed to convince their parents to buy them a cat during pick-up time. The campers leave happy, and the camp makes some money.

We have a joke in my family that if you even think about wanting another cat, one will appear in the driveway. Or a friend will find an abandoned one in a box on the side of the street. Or the neighbor's cat will have babies. Somehow, we say, cats know when you'll be most vulnerable to their advances.

At the time, we had one family cat, the least amount of animals—or even cats—we'd ever had, following the death of our old dog and then our other cat. The one we had was mostly feral. Whacked at our hands and hissed when we tried to pet her. Growled at our food. Slept by herself at night. We were starved for an animal that actually liked being around us, so the universe delivered—in the form of the six kittens.

I talked to my mom on the phone one night.

"If none of them are right, then I don't have to take one," I said.

My parents placed a lot of pressure on me when I told them about the cats. To my surprise, they didn't seem opposed to the idea of another one. But my track record wasn't great. There was our feral cat, who I rescued when I was in high school from a boy in my class who found her in a bag by his house and planned to take her to the pound—the first animal I ever got to choose myself that I could name and that was solely mine. I had grand visions of her being the best cat. In reality, she only really liked my dad, and that was because he ignored her, a trait cats seem inclined to appreciate.

I had to promise I would choose a better cat this time.

My mom told me to "make sure it likes being handled." If there were none in the litter of six that liked being pet and picked up, then I would have to leave the kittens to their stray, forest life.

I knew about Gus before I had a chance to see him; he had already escaped multiple times in the first few days upon entering the enclosure where he'd live for the summer. He was the sole inhabitant of the crate deemed "Pet Farm Time Out," a space made for misbehaving kittens during their playtime with the kids. I had a feeling the activity runners were trying to be diplomatic, but really it should have been called "Houdini Time Out." All the counselors talked about the quick kitten that liked to take advantage of the opportunities an open door presented. Maybe it's indicative of a more deep-seated issue around staking my claim on things that everyone else starts to like after I'd been talking about them forever, like those people who comment "First!" on Instagram pictures because they want to seem cool, but hearing about Gus piqued my interest. Deep down, I wanted to be cool enough to lay claim on the enigmatic cat.

Every camp session, I led the Photo and Journalism class. The slots never filled up completely. Only a few children wanted to take photos and write for the newsletter that went out to every camper and parent biweekly when there were other activities like fencing and archery and vaulting to choose from. Even if I managed to convince kids to take the activity, the mix usually consisted of first-year campers or kids more suited to internet-based hobbies than climbing a rock wall for an hour. Whatever free time I had open throughout the day, I spent mostly at Pet Farm, attempting to force a bond with a barn kitten that wanted nothing more than to get out of there.

"The gray one. The one that likes to escape," I told the counselor who ran Pet Farm.

"Houdini? That one is crazy," she said. "Are you sure you want him?"

I did. And not just because he was the most popular. That did help, but he also climbed into my lap every time I went to Pet Farm and played with the kids without a hiss. Gus was well-tempered and an even mix of rambunctious and cuddly.

Campers came and went as the summer went on, and whenever I had a bad day, I went to Pet Farm to hang out with Gus, who more and more felt like mine. When kids gripped a little too tightly around his neck trying to hold him, I said, "My turn," and plucked Gus from their greedy hands. When one claimed, "I'm going to take Houdini home!" I reminded him that the other cats were much better.

I was on my day off the time Gus climbed a forty-foot pine tree. Everyone was so used to his antics by then—and unwilling to take the time to get him down because it was dinner time and he wouldn't listen anyway—that he stayed up in the tree through the whole meal. My best friend, who had taken a job at the camp with me, was the only one who stayed at the base of the tree, missing dinner, while Gus swayed on a branch. From what I gathered when I got back that night, he was content to watch the birds from that vantage point, and came flying back down the tree trunk when he was satisfied.

I had been at the Grand Canyon with another counselor when it happened: a guy a year younger than me told me as we sat in a horrible Mexican restaurant that I was "more attractive in person" than in the photos we all saw before meeting each other. And then proceeded to rate me on a scale of one to ten. He lessened the blow by asking what my rating would be of him. It would take me months after camp ended to realize how messed up that conversation had been. Months after giving up more of myself than I should have.

The next day, I held onto Gus a little tighter. Maybe because he could have hurt himself in that pine tree. Maybe because I'd been hurt a little myself.

Two weeks before the end of camp, I was told that Gus had been promised to someone else.

Apparently the promise was made not knowing that Houdini was the tabby I had specified. It came at the worst part of the summer—and that's including the first week when I had bed bugs. A new batch of campers had arrived, and my co-counselor and I ended up with the quote-unquote "worst cabin our superiors had ever seen in their combined experience of over thirty years." There were language barriers, and manipulation, and twins who teamed up to scream at us in the middle of the night when we told them to go to bed.

I'd never wanted to fight a sixteen-year-old until I learned that my cat was going home with one.

"I'll pay you for him," I tried.

"No, I want him."

Underneath the counselors were counselors-in-training (CITs), sixteen-year-olds who had previously attended the camp learning how to be counselors in the hopes that at eighteen, they'd get summer jobs there. Sometimes when I'm walking down the street and come across a group of teenagers who are very obviously of the cool variety, I get nervous. As a near 25-year-old. I think it's a pretty common thing, some kind of leftover conditioning from being made fun of. I tense, knowing how cruel their comments can be. Envious of how confidently they already carry themselves at sixteen.

That was this kid. I liked the other CITs. Would even go so far as to say that they liked hanging around me, even if it was because I let them in on some camp secrets and didn't treat them like servants as the other counselors tended to do. But this one had a high-and-mighty attitude. Acted superior, fighting with us over rules because he'd attended the camp his whole life. It was odd, being confronted with someone six years younger than me who already understood the power of privilege. His parents could afford to send him to camp every summer since he was five. He deserved his choice of cat because he'd been there longer. He didn't need my hard-earned money. He just wanted the most popular cat.

And although the lines of appropriateness were blurred at this job (I mean, so many. So, so many), I wasn't about to freak out in front of people. I considered it a point of pride that I had yet to cry that summer. It seemed everyone did: We worked almost 24/7, felt grimy constantly, and dealt with moody kids and sometimes even moodier coworkers all living within the same area for three months. But even though I kept my composure, when the director saw me later that day, he gave me two consecutive free hours. It was unheard of. That was the amount of time we got off every night; he'd basically given me an extra night off. He had no idea about me losing Gus, but I must've looked near breaking.

My best friend lived apart from the kids, with the other counselors who ran the horse activities. Their jobs had them up at 5:00 a.m., so they stayed in the lodge up a hill. No one else was allowed up in those rooms, for the obvious reasons that young adults aren't allowed in unregulated places. That day, though, I plopped down on my best friend's bed and cried.

I called my mom in the middle of it. Sobbed about losing my cat. About the ten-year-olds who'd made the last two weeks feel like a month.

"I don't know how you've done it all summer," she said in the way that moms do over the phone, like they're crying along with you. But I didn't want compliments on how I'd gotten through the summer when what pushed me over the edge was not getting the cat I wanted.

My parents listened while I hiccuped through my explanation of the asshole teenager unwilling to even listen to how I'd been bonding with Houdini the whole summer. Nothing could be done, short of involving the people who employed me, and I valued my reputation too much to do that. I kept asking the kid if he didn't have the heart to understand what had happened and pick a different cat for himself, but I knew nothing would work. I couldn't go back to Pet Farm after that. Not to say goodbye to Gus. Not to play with him again.

The CITs left a day before we counselors did. Gus had been taken in the back of the teenager's parents' car without me noticing.

I threw myself into the deep cleaning required of us before we were set free. I was sweeping the endless amounts of dirt from the most isolated cabin, farthest from any of the main buildings when I heard it. Someone shouting my name.

"We've been looking for you!" one of my friends explained as she came running up to me, out of breath. "They're bringing him back. You're getting your cat."

I dropped everything. Made her promise she was sure about what she'd heard.

"Yeah, he's already back," the Pet Farm counselor told me when I found her. "They took him home and said their other cat didn't get along with him and that he was too crazy."

I ran through the main area of the camp, telling everyone who would listen that I got my cat back. It felt a little like everyone got him back, since so many of my fellow counselors had argued with the CIT on my behalf and seen how much he didn't care. In the end, I didn't even have to pay the $25.

My parents admitted they had no idea why I was so upset about losing Gus that day I called them crying. They did know how hard the summer was, if not all the details and all the ups and downs, the new friends and blurred lines. Once they saw him, though, they understood how the little barn cat drew me in, and why it hurt so much to lose him. I left camp that summer not exactly having "found myself." But I did leave with a cat that I thought I had lost, and instead found in the end, despite everything. Even if Gus is cooler than me, and still sometimes lives up to his old escape artist moniker by trying to flee the house, I believe he is meant to be my cat after all.

CATTERS

Courtney Stevenson

NOCHE

Julia S. Owens

Noche,
the Mayor of
New Queen Lane

T here's a special feeling when a cat likes you, and Noche had this figured out. He stroked the egos of many pedestrians in East Falls, Philadelphia, and he was known as the mayor of New Queen Lane.

I first met Noche when I had the honor of his presence on my porch one evening, shortly after I'd moved to the neighborhood. As he peered at me through my glass front door, I texted a picture of him to my sister. She texted back, "He has chosen you."

The next day, I scrolled through the social media site Nextdoor, a habit I enjoy for its pettiness. A post revealed that Noche had graced someone else's porch recently, and several neighbors confirmed he was a special outdoor cat who does, in fact, have a human to care for him. I no longer felt chosen, but the mayor introducing himself to me felt like a warm welcome to my new community.

Some time later, when Noche's owner posted that he was missing, I, along with other Noche fans, vowed to keep an eye out for him. I watched his owner save him from being cooped up at the house of a neighbor who mistook him for a stray. She told me the same neighbor did the same thing to Noche about ten years earlier because she didn't believe cats should be outdoors. I felt guilty for not knowing he was held hostage when I could've freed him from his prison.

Noche's owner also said that due to his old age, he would become an indoor cat in the winter for the first time in his life. I imagined he would hold court from a cat patio during the chilly winter days, and that I would visit him to hear him gripe about retirement.

His owner never got around to the cat patio, and Noche went to stay with someone else for the winter. She said that one day his sitter left the patio door open, and Noche took his chance, never to be seen again. Well of course, not by the residents near New Queen Lane anyway. I'm sure he's out there making the pedestrians in his new neighborhood feel just as special.

I'LL TAKE THAT AS A COMMENT

Nicholas Beckett

CARTOONS' COOLEST CATS

Ed Kemp

There have been many cartoon cats throughout the years. Some have been in starring roles, like Felix, possibly our first cartoon cat, or Fritz, the cat whose self-titled movie scored an X rating in 1972, while others, like Azrael from *The Smurfs* or *Pinocchio*'s Figaro, were just supporting characters. All cats are cool, that's without question, but only the coolest of the cool cats made my cut.

5. Tom from Tom and Jerry

Tom's a lovable loser, similar to the Chicago Cubs before they won the World Series back in 2016. I like Tom, but let's face it, he's a dud. He's constantly getting outsmarted, or even worse, out-muscled, by a much smaller creature further down the food chain. In the end, though, I guess it's a good thing because if this cartoon played out like real life, it could have been a short and gruesome cartoon series.

4. Chester Cheetah

"It's not easy being cheesy" is almost enough on its own to land Chester on this list, but looking back on old commercials, that wasn't the only sick bar our cartoon Cheetah spit back in the day. Many commercials from my youth had him reciting rhyme after cheesy rhyme, sounding like some sort of beatnik poet, all while being voiced by a Tone Loc impersonator. And if his poetry skills weren't enough, animators had him wear sneakers and sunglasses to emphasize just how cool he really was. Also, Cheetos are way better than Frosted Flakes, which gives Chester the edge over that bandana-wearing, sugary cereal–selling tiger.

3. Snowball II

While not the most major character in the series—often losing screen time to that scene-stealing show-off, Santa's Little Helper—she is the Simpsons' family cat, and the show is the greatest cartoon ever, so ipso facto she's here on the list. But let's not forget about the fact that she does totally belong here. She did, after all, save Homer from that burning treehouse while "man's best friend" turned his cowardly back. Also, there was the time she gained a bunch of weight by moonlighting with another family and getting double fed, something that my first cat really did. MacGregor was an indoor/outdoor cat that would sometimes disappear for a week or two at a time, often coming home smelling of smoke, but we could never really figure out why. We theorized that she had a side family that had a campfire or chain smoked Marlboro Reds or something. Well, after she died, we saw flyers from someone looking for a missing cat fitting my cat's description. My mom called and talked to the "other" family, and it turned out that our theory was spot on: our calico cat led a double life with another family for years leading up to her passing.

2. Sylvester

Sly gets a bad rap for hunting the cute, sweet, and catchphrase-spewing Tweety Bird, but it is not his fault. *He's a cat!* He's predisposed to want to hunt birds. It's in his DNA. No, I blame the lady of the house, Granny, for all of this. She's an adult and should know better. Besides, does she really want a cat that's not going to protect her house from scurrying or flying creatures? Oscar voters noticed the plight that Sylvester was in and awarded three of his cartoons with Academy Awards, validating his spot on this list of cartoons' all-time coolest cats.

1. Garfield

By far the cattiest of all cartoon cats and just the coolest of the cool. All he wants to do is eat and sleep and has nothing but utter disdain for his roommates. In all fairness though, he was saddled with two lousy ones. Odie is a dork and Arbuckle is even worse. Jon is lucky his pets can't fend for themselves, otherwise I'm sure they'd leave his sorry ass. Look, Garfield hates Mondays and downs lasagna like he lives in North Jersey. There's a reason why the cartoon is named after him—and why he's top cat on my list.

JUST VISITING

Craig Wenner

*I*n the autumn of 2001, my family received a visitor. Friendly and with courage disguised by her petite frame, this presumably stray long-haired calico won the affections of everyone in my household with her frequent visits (made all the more frequent via a steady offering of kibble on the patio). She spent afternoons sunbathing outside the back door and providing services as jobsite supervisor while my dad tinkered in the toolshed. She could always be relied upon to offer an after-school greeting at the bus stop, too, her belly and green eyes pointed toward the sky.

It should have surprised no one when this cat one day decided to slip into our house, chasing down an especially aromatic dinner my mom was preparing. After some initial reluctance (likely feigned) from my dad, the cat was allowed to come and go from the house as she pleased. She was set up with a folded blanket as a bed in the dining room for whenever she visited, and food and water bowls in a regular spot.

Sometime during this part-time roommate situation, we learned that the cat was, in fact, not a stray. She had a name and a home. Clam lived a few houses down and across the street from us, but she rarely, if ever, spent any time there, as far as we could tell. We learned that Clam lived life on the edge as an outdoor cat, having been struck by a car on more than one occasion, garnering her the nickname Calamity Jane. This revelation ultimately changed nothing, aside from giving us a name to call her. She showed up on her own schedule, waited to be let in, and left when she saw fit, never overstaying her welcome. Clam was friendly and playful, and it always felt special that she chose us. Reflecting now, it seems entirely possible, and admittedly even likely, that we were just one of several households Clam frequented. She was clearly smart and possessed a strong survival instinct. I don't think that would have changed much of anything in terms of our relationship, though it is a funny scenario to imagine, and would have only added to her already impressive lore.

Eventually, though, Clam stopped coming. It wasn't a gradual thing, but all at once. I don't think my parents had ever talked to Clam's owners about her, so approaching them to ask where she'd gone would have seemed pretty strange. I think we must've hoped, best-case, that her owners simply stopped letting her outside. Time passed, and we stopped wondering. Her makeshift bed was put away, and her bowls returned to their pre-Clam circulation.

Months passed, and on Halloween night, after I had concluded my haunt of the neighborhood, I returned home to evaluate my haul. I settled down in the living room where my dad was watching TV between his trips to the door to offer candy to the trick-or-treaters. As I sat on the floor separating and categorizing my candy (chocolate, gummy, hard), a group of too-old trick-or-treaters came to the door. I watched, disappointed, as the last of the Reese's cups was hastily snatched up.

"Your cat's out here," one member of the group remarked. Before my dad could reply, Clam scurried in through the still-open door and tore through the house toward the kitchen where I found her patiently waiting where her bowls would have been, as if she had never left.

My memory of Clam's saga ends here. I've included two photos of Clam taken between autumn 2001 and February 2002. Ahead of writing this, I asked my parents if they were able to recall anything further, but they remembered even fewer specifics than me. My memory of her is most certainly skewed by the rose-tinted and embellished recollection of the eight-year-old me who experienced it, but I think that only adds to the storybook feeling of this tale. Thanks for choosing us, Clam.

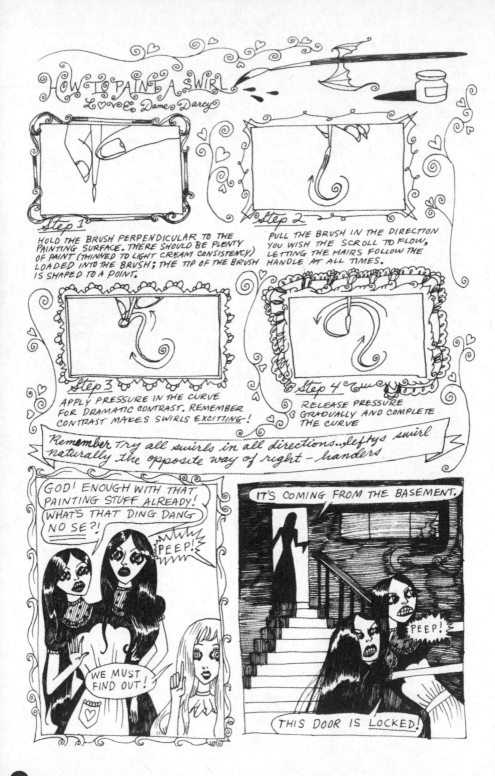

HOW TO PAINT A SWIRL
Love Dame Darcy

Step 1
HOLD THE BRUSH PERPENDICULAR TO THE PAINTING SURFACE. THERE SHOULD BE PLENTY OF PAINT (THINNED TO LIGHT CREAM CONSISTENCY) LOADED INTO THE BRUSH; THE TIP OF THE BRUSH IS SHAPED TO A POINT.

Step 2
PULL THE BRUSH IN THE DIRECTION YOU WISH THE SCROLL TO FLOW, LETTING THE HAIRS FOLLOW THE HANDLE AT ALL TIMES.

Step 3
APPLY PRESSURE IN THE CURVE FOR DRAMATIC CONTRAST. REMEMBER CONTRAST MAKES SWIRLS EXCITING!

Step 4
RELEASE PRESSURE GRADUALLY AND COMPLETE THE CURVE

Remember Try all swirls in all directions...leftys swirl naturally the opposite way of right-handers

GOD! ENOUGH WITH THAT PAINTING STUFF ALREADY! WHAT'S THAT DING DANG NOISE?!

PEEP!

WE MUST FIND OUT!

IT'S COMING FROM THE BASEMENT.

PEEP!

THIS DOOR IS LOCKED!

201

GETTING TRAINED

Ellen Muehlberger

hen we first went to the animal shelter to adopt cats, we knew only that we wanted two neutered boy cats. Trouble was, there was a whole room of them, all gorgeous in their various ways. But one cat was gorgeous and loud. Wearing a fancy black-and-white tuxedo, he called out to me as I passed his cage, saying something that sounded like an expectant question: "Well??" Once I stopped to say hello and held my finger up to the cage for him to sniff, he hit me with the double question: "Well-well??" and it was all over. There at the shelter his name was Dickens, but when he got home we called him Dodds, after a favorite street we had lived on in southern Indiana.

The other cat who came home with us that day was Tiny, a tabby who was, in fact, a bit larger than Dodds and a bit less social. We got the sense over time that maybe Tiny had been ignored, or left alone a lot, wherever he lived before he came to the shelter. Once he was in our house, he wasn't quite sure what we were, or even what he was supposed to be. But Dodds had the duties and rights of a cat down to a science, and he spent the first few months of his time with us training Tiny how to cat. You could see Tiny working it out: *Oh, these people feed you—they're going to feed me? Oh, they let you sit on their laps—maybe I could try that sometime? Oh, we can sleep by them?* All of these are things that no human being could have explained to him but that Dodds just showed him. Tiny loved him for it.

Dodds also showed us. The minute either one of us did a thing that he liked, he would latch onto that thing and then figure out how to set up the circumstances for us to do it again. Mostly, it had to do with treats. Dodds figured out pretty quickly that we in our house adhere to the Universal Feline Conventions, the most important of which is § 136.4(a), Cat on Lap, Must Not Disrupt. So, if Dodds had gotten on a lap, then he received some kind of compensation for having to get off of the lap, like a piece of food. It did not take long before Dodds would get on any lap, at any opportunity, because he knew that at some point, getting off the lap would mean getting a piece of food. He can seem like a cuddler, but in fact he's just pragmatic: lapsitting is the way to make kibble appear, and he works that angle any time he can.

It would have continued in this way, just lapsitting and little treats here and there, if we hadn't had friends over to dinner one night. Both of our friends have dogs whom they trained— the humans had actually met in an obedience class!—and one of them, Catherine, said, "You know what? Dodds is probably trainable. He's really food motivated, and I bet you could teach him tricks."

By the end of that very night, Dodds had learned to step over a forearm laid on the floor in order to get to a piece of food, and it has been a very steep trajectory since then. Now, he reports to the kitchen every evening when we are cooking dinner because that is the time that his practice sessions occur. He leaps over extended forearms held high off the floor; he jumps through hoops made by just putting your hands together; he sits and then spins 360 degrees (clockwise or counterclockwise) by just watching the flick of a human wrist to the left or to the right. He lines up on your left side and then slinks between your legs, one then the other, as you take five steps forward. He's a show cat, and he runs his tricks together one after the other so that our house has essentially become his agility course.

But on top of this showy stuff, he's also still working on other ways to acclimate us to having him. Neither of the humans in the house is exactly clear on how it started, but somehow, there is now a rule that if Dodds "catches" one of us in the basement, we are required to stand at the bottom of the stairs, wait for him to join us, then yell "Thunder Road!" while he bolts up the stairs; then he gets a few pieces of food. Sometimes, days pass between one Thunder Road and the next. On the weekends, though, we go up and down the stairs a lot, so he catches us a lot, sometimes three or four or five times in a row. If my partner goes downstairs and Dodds hears it from another room, he will often sneak through the house and down the stairs to wait for her to realize that he's caught her down there: She must execute a Thunder Road.

Dodds is a senior cat, but not super-senior and still very hale, so we are expecting to be taught more tricks in the coming years. In fact, this started out as an essay about how we trained our cat, but now I have to admit that he trained us.

OFFICIAL MINUTES OF KITTY CAT CLUB

Kay Coster

April 1, 2023

Denver, CO

Members in Attendance:

Veronica, Age 8

Aunt Kay, Age 57

The meeting was called to order at 11:05 a.m. Because we do not have a quorum (missing Aunt Kim, Uncle Paul, cousins Cher and Bonnie) we cannot take any votes today. Both members are wearing their official Kitty Cat Club cat ears.

First order of business: Veronica wants to know if we've ever talked about her best friend Maddie. "We have a lot in common, but she really bugs me sometimes."

Second order of business: Arrived at Just Cats Store (and adoptions) for their fifth birthday party. Greeted by Sophie, a fourteen-year-old ginger who reluctantly let us pet her. Veronica notes for the record, "Tangerine would be a better name."

Third order of business: Met Mackenzie, another ginger girl who showed us her beautiful belly, but we were warned, "Don't try it." Mackenzie only likes head scratches. Noted. Scratched Mackenzie's head. No other cats appear to be present today.

Fourth order of business: Veronica has a slice of birthday cake with "the best frosting I've ever had." She passes on also having a cupcake because they don't have enough sprinkles. Shopping commences. Items purchased:

1. Stickers (cat/cactus, cool kitty with sunglasses, teeny silhouette cats) and Ninja Cat pin for Veronica

2. Pineapple-shaped catnip toy, assorted cat food, and cat toys for Aunt Kay's cats: Ernest, Sabrina, and Prunella

Several people complimented our cat ears. The store owner gave us a birthday gift. We said goodbye to Sophie/Tangerine and left.

Sixth order of business: Lunch at the nearby deli where we couldn't wait to see what was in our gift bag: more cat food plus a photo of a cat inside a thank-you note. Veronica is certain that everyone who received a gift bag got a different cat photo. She has named hers Tigerball and he is her new pet cat. She has always wanted a cat and he's going to live in her bedroom with her. This is an exciting and unexpected development.

Over lunch, the following business was discussed:

1. What is your favorite name for a cat? Veronica: *Mango*, Aunt Kay: *Francisco*

2. What is your favorite animal that isn't a cat? Veronica: *Orangutan*, Aunt Kay: *Chimpanzee*

3. What is your favorite animal name to say? Veronica: *Orangutan*, Aunt Kay: *Cow*

4. Members mooed and giggled for a little bit.

5. Watched a video of a cat and dog that like to cuddle with each other when their people are gone. It was super cute. Lots of squealing.

6. "Strawberries make me puke," notes Veronica who picks them out of her fruit salad.

7. The conversation turns to hobbies. Veronica likes to knit and draw (people, not animals.) Aunt Kay likes photography and reading. Veronica proclaims, "I think you might be Future Me!"

8. Cousin Richard is sad that he wasn't admitted into Kitty Cat Club. Veronica says that this is because when he came to visit their house recently, he acted like their dog (Indy) was his. Aunt Kay suggested that maybe this is because he really loves animals and so maybe his membership is worth reconsidering. After all, he lives with a dog named Dingo and a cat named Potato. Veronica says she will think about it and reminds Aunt Kay that we can't vote on anything today anyway.

Bought cake pops. Veronica notes, "I cannot wait to brag to [older brother] about how much fun we had today."

Meeting adjourned at 1:30 p.m. Cat ears removed until the next meeting.

MY CAT IS NAMED MYNAH

Anna Lehr Mueser

My cat is named Mynah, after the Central and South Asian talking bird. She's a small, black tripod cat, with long silky fur, and a hopping gait. Like a pigeon or a dove, she often makes small burbling sounds as she skips along. The idea of naming a cat after a bird seemed hilarious to me and my partner, and it also allowed us to call her Little My, like the mischievous Tove Jansson character who rides around in a teacup and tears apart Moominmamma's knitting. My partner and I like to think that while Mynah is curled inside a bin of tablecloths watching us cook, she, like the moomins—whose adventures often highlight moominpappa's fragile masculinity, and whose family is defined by an open and welcoming inclusivity—is actually offering a radical and subversive critique of the heteronormative bourgeois family.

As a general rule, Mynah does not sleep in our bed, she almost never climbs into our laps, and she seldom accepts the cuddles I am always trying to give. Between the enthusiastic feeding frenzy of her breakfast, which is often preceded by half an hour of her yelling for our attention, and the dinnertime repeat, Mynah mostly sleeps in a cardboard cat-scratching box and plays on her own with paper bags full of catnip toys. This is to say that, unlike the moomins, Mynah is a bit distant and cold.

In the fall of 2020, I took the first substantial trip of my doctoral research, to the Catskills, where I am studying the history of New York City's rural drinking water supply. We'd discovered that traveling with the cat was easier and less expensive than trying to find a cat sitter for two weeks. Plus, we had the misguided impression that it was "good" for Mynah to experience new places, and perhaps hunt a mouse out in the country. So, Mynah was coming on the research trip too. At the last minute, my partner had to go to their parents' house, and so Mynah and I set off on our own.

In what must have seemed like pointless torture, Mynah was tricked into her crate, buckled into a car which also included a desk chair—a detailed analysis of photos of the one-room schoolhouse I'd rented suggested that there were no comfortable work chairs in which I could sit for hours processing each day's photographs and scans—and a box of CSA veggies I couldn't stand to abandon, and we hit the road.

Arriving in the Catskills at night is like arriving in any other remote rural place in the dark: your view shrinks down to the pool of a porch light and the long angles of your headlights. It was dim and overcast and just before the new moon, and the darkness was deep. The mountains blocked out much of the sky. One-intersection villages with just one or two dim orange streetlights were long passed by the time I reached my destination. The night was dark and quiet; what in the daytime would be welcoming and warm felt cold, strange.

That night, when we arrived at the schoolhouse some six hours after leaving home, Mynah's small yowling presence immediately warmed the place, making it feel homelike to me.

Still, a strange place is still strange. The house had the doggish smell of rentals that allow you to bring your pets, and instead of two people, Mynah had only one of us to ignore. I felt relieved when I'd finally carried in the veggies and the desk chair and the suitcase of clothing designed to make me look equally competent in a museum archive and in the remote woods where a special permit would allow me to hike along the reservoirs that supply New York City's water. Mynah felt differently. To a small, three-legged cat, the schoolhouse was one large, dog-smelling, unfamiliar space, full of cold chairs, a troublingly hairy rug, and a fridge that turned its compressor on and off at forty-minute intervals. She was not having a good time, and ran from corner to corner crying out in confusion.

That night, lonely and exhausted and as yet unsure how to turn on the heat, I crawled into bed. Mynah, who usually sleeps all night in her cardboard box—which I packed for her so she could refuse my company just as well in the Catskills as at home—jumped up onto the bed. It was a high bed: my feet couldn't reach the floor while sitting on it. For a cat with only one back leg, it was quite an achievement. I could hear her grab onto the mattress with her claws and pull herself up. She came trotting up to me, picking her way over the rumpled covers, and settled beside me, tucked against the pillow. She spent the night curled against my chest, her head resting on my arm. In a combination of anxiety about the new space and delight at feline affection, I basically didn't sleep. In the morning, Mynah gave me a dazed, tired look as if to say, *you're not the only one!*

Every night for nine lonely nights, Mynah slept beside me, her soft snuffles a comforting sound. In the morning, she nosed my hands as soon as she could tell I was awake, her little always-wet nose telling me to get up and feed her. I spent each day driving around to my research sites, taking pictures and making notes, obsessively reading interpretive signs, and trying to comprehend the meaning, and the making of meaning, in these places. When I came back, Mynah greeted me with a mixture of relief and boredom, but each night she snuggled against me, and we both felt at home.

CAT-LIKE

Jo-Jo Sherrow

CONTRIBUTORS

Katie Haegele is a writer and editor from Philadelphia. She has published several books, most of them memoirs or collections of essays, and many zines. Her most recent books are *Kitchen Witch: Natural Remedies and Crafts for Home, Health, and Beauty* and *Spiritbox*, an art book of poems that are kind of like memes. Katie is a proud bisexual lady who runs a zine library with her partner, cares for animals at a wildlife clinic, and enjoys the catharsis of making extremely loud noise music. https://TheLalaTheory.com.

Mocha Ishibashi currently teaches violin at Little Bow Music and Waseca Montessori, and has performed and recorded with artists like Herbie Hancock, Diana Krall, Christian McBride, CeeLo Green, and of Montreal.

Joe Genaro is a songwriter and musician from southeastern Pennsylvania, best known as the guitarist for the Philadelphia-based punk band the Dead Milkmen, of which he is a founding member.

Melissa Eismann took photos of her cats Kevin and Yui on 35 mm film. Melissa can be found on Instagram @WaxLeaf.

Andrew Keller is a recent convert to cat-lover status. He really had no idea how great cats were until one showed up in his backyard and wormed her way into his heart. Andrew writes music under the name Snow Caps (@snow__caps).

Gina Brandolino lives in Ann Arbor, Michigan with her partner Ellen and Dodds, a very dapper tuxedo cat who calls all the shots. She owns more kitty blocks than dining room chairs and more cat beds than human beds (also, the tuxedo cat prefers the human beds and gets to choose his spot while the humans sleep around him). She carries her two beloved deceased cats in her heart, which works well, because the tuxedo doesn't like to be picked up.

Heidi Moreno is an author/illustrator based in Los Angeles, California. She also works under the name Heidiroo and runs a small shop. Her work has an abundance of cats and other creatures living in her spooky universe. You can find her going on walks in her neighborhood with treats in her pockets to give to the community cats.

Key K. Bird (they/her) is a fiction writer whose stories have been published online and in print, most recently in the *Rumpus*. Key lives with their best friend and an always beckoning, in-progress novel.

Christa Dippel works under the artist name Defectivepudding. She is a self-taught illustrator and visual artist and has been pursuing art professionally for several years now. Her works are primarily created in colored pencil and graphite, drawing most of her inspiration from vintage media, toys, and clothes, in addition to a fascination with wildlife and nature. As a result, many of her pieces have a nostalgically sweet appearance, even while exploring subjects that are melancholy.

Mardou is a cartoonist and long-form graphic novelist who lives in St. Louis, Missouri with her family. She began making minicomics after getting her BA in English Literature from the University of Wales in 1998. Working in both fiction and autobiography, Mardou's comics explore interior experiences such as mental illness, emotional dynamics within families, and healing from trauma.

River Katz is a genderflexible kitty disguised as a human artist in the 3D world. They are the comic artist for *Do Not Pet: A Service Dog's Graphic Tale Vol. 1*, cover designer and contributor to *True Trans Bike Rebel*, and contributor to other zines like *Cat Party* and *We've All Got Baggage*. River enjoys making art related to gender, cannabis, magic and spirituality, music, mental health, fur-people, and occasional fan art. When not doodling away on their ipad, they're designing handmade tarot cards, collaging vision boards, obsessively sketchbooking, writing music, thinking up zine ideas, or teaching themself animation.

Jackie Soro (she/they) is a performer and artist based in Philadelphia. She enjoys improvising, being outside, good books, crafts, gardening, singing, and speaking in a loud voice. Jackie recently finished their Saturn Return, and in the spirit of that transition, has declined to list past accomplishments here. Instead, she would like to invite advice and anecdotes about how to create a solid, sustainable lifestyle as an artist living under capitalism (email: HelloJSoro@gmail.com).

Rebecca Bayuk is a Brit born and raised not far from Brontë country, now living near Washington, D.C. At five she declared she wanted to be an "arthur"; since then, she has written in various forms, with an emphasis on poetry, short stories, and essays, plus a four-year stint blogging about history for teenagers. She has also learned how to pronounce author. Rebecca is a typography nerd, (slow) runner, and is partial to an occasional kitchen disco. Cats she's owned have yet to be impressed by her dance moves, but she remains undeterred.

Kelsey Stewart is an artist living in South Philadelphia. She's a storyteller who has performed onstage with First Person Arts and Rose Valley Storytelling, and she draws slice-of-life comics, which she shares on Instagram. She loves cloud appreciation, not-quite-green-thumb gardening, and pool parties. You can find her art on Instagram at @ KelseyStewartComics or look her up on Patreon.

Keet Geniza is a queer nonbinary illustrator, zinester, cartoonist, and youth arts facilitator from Manila, Philippines. They love cats but are very shy around them. Their works and process can be seen on their blog at https://MakeshiftLove.com and on their Instagram @ MakeshiftLove. Keet currently lives, works, and waves at cats in Toronto.

Justin Duerr was born in 1976 and grew up in rural Pennsylvania. In the early '90s, he dropped out of high school and moved to Philadelphia, where he still lives. For twenty years, the majority of his work has revolved around an ongoing storyline, the plot of which deals with the big issues facing life-forms, dualities, and the seeking of transcendent states of nonbeing even while alive. The interconnecting series of scroll drawings now contains over 34 installments and spans over one hundred feet in length. In 2018, he wrote *The Temple of Silence: Forgotten Works and Worlds of Herbert Crowley*, a monograph and art book about the British visionary artist. In 2022, he wrote and compiled a book of art by mediumistic Philadelphia artist Renee Leshner called *RENEE LESHNER: Conqueror of the Evil Eye.* https://JustinDuerr.com

Ivan Dellinger is a writer, artist, and performer living in Philadelphia. He has been drawing *The Crime Cats* daily since April 26, 2022. You can find more crime cats on his Instagram @capybaras and find his other work at https://linktr.ee/capybarazz.

Joe Biel is a self-made autistic publisher and filmmaker who draws origins, inspiration, and methods from punk rock. Biel is the founder and CEO of Microcosm Publishing, *Publishers Weekly's* #1 fastest-growing publisher of 2022. Biel has been featured in *Time Magazine, Publishers Weekly, Art of Autism, Reading Glasses, Bulletproof Radio, Spectator* (Japan), *G33K* (Korea), and *Maximum Rocknroll*, as well as on NPR and PBS. Biel is the author of *A People's Guide to Publishing: Building a Successful, Sustainable, Meaningful Book Business, Good Trouble: Building a Successful Life & Business on the Spectrum, Manspressions: Decoding Men's Behavior, Make a Zine, The CIA Makes Science Fiction Unexciting, Proud to be Retarded, Bicycle Culture Rising*, and more. Biel is the director of five feature films and hundreds of short films, including *Aftermass: Bicycling in a Post-Critical Mass Portland, $100 & a T-Shirt*, and the Groundswell film series. Biel lives in Portland, OR.

Joe Carlough is a queer artist from Philadelphia. He runs the zine press and DIY record label Displaced Snail Zines n' Records, through which he releases his own work, as well as the writing and music of Katie Haegele, Spencer Moody (Murder City Devils), Joe Jack Talcum (the Dead Milkmen), lauren.napier, Gina Brandolino, and dozens of other occasional collaborators. He's released roughly 30,000 copies of 330 unique zines. His first book with Microcosm Publishing, *The Queer Affirmations Coloring Book*, was released in November 2023.

Rachel Blythe Udell and **Jeremy Newman** are full-time cat people and also make art. They collaborate on drawings, mixed media works, and films. Known for her textile sculptures and installations, Udell earned a BA in Art History from the University of Pennsylvania and studied Art Therapy at the School of the Art Institute of Chicago. She received a 2023 fellowship from the New Jersey State Council on the Arts in sculpture. Newman makes both feature documentary and short experimental films. He earned an MFA in Media Arts from the Ohio State University. Newman is Associate Professor of Communications at Stockton University. They live in Mantua, New Jersey.

Nicholas Beckett has spent a lifetime avoiding success. It's going pretty well so far. After drawing and painting one thousand protesting figures to no acclaim, he thought he was finished with the project, but the world has continued to deliver grievances and so the protesting never ends. He has been known to draw cats and has had the great honor of drawing for Katie in the past. You can find out more than you need to know on: https://SaintBeckett.net, https://facebook.com/Rosicholas, and on Instagram @ SaintBuckett.

delphadae, a.k.a. Ashley, is an artist living in northeastern Pennsylvania. She enjoys making comics and illustrations with inks, watercolor paint, and colored pencils. The subject matter ranges from the simple and cute, to mental illness and introspection.

Alison Lee Chapman is an illustrator living and working in Philadelphia, Pennsylvania. She finds her inspiration in Wissahickon Valley Park, small neighborhood gardens, and watching her kids grow up. You can see more of her work at https://AlisonLeeChapman.com or on Instagram @WolfTreeStudio.

Steven Svymbersky is the founder of Quimby's Bookstore in Chicago (1991–1997) and the founder/owner of Quimby's Bookstore NYC (2016–) in Brooklyn. Between bookstores, he worked for nineteen years as the head technician at Boom Chicago improv theater in Amsterdam. Everywhere he goes, there are always cats.

Cartoonist **Dame Darcy**, with fifty plus graphic novels (and ongoing), is published internationally. Starting in the '90s zine scene, her comic *Meat Cake* has been compiled into a five-hundred-page book by Fantagraphics called *The Meat Cake Bible*. It spans her 25-year career as cartoonist, writer, and illustrator of graphic novels and has now been optioned as a feature film by North of Two in Los Angeles. She has had the honor of working with greats such as Alan Moore, Poppy Z. Brite, Holt, DC, Marvel, Penguin, and others. New releases include *Vegan Love* (Skyhorse, 2017) and *Lady Killers* (Harper Collins, 2017), which she illustrated, and her autobiography *Hi Jax & Hi Jinx* (Feral House, 2018) with accompanying screenplay.

Amanda Laughtland and Mr. Cat live in the suburbs of Seattle, where she grades papers and occasionally makes zines.

Mellen Reinbold is a freelance illustrator who currently lives and works in Allentown, Pennsylvania. When she's not making art, you can find her foraging for wild edible plants or playing with her dog, Potato. To see more of her work, find her on Instagram:@MellenMade or visit her website: https://MellenMade.com.

Nicole @NightOwlDesigns and Nicole @TapedOffTV made a collage tribute to their cat Nova. **Nicole**[2] co-own the South Street Art Mart, an artist-run retail shop located in the heart of Philly's South Street shopping district. With DIY roots and punk sensibility, the Art Mart is home to over 180 Philly-area artists and makers (and some from around the country). All products are created by independent artists and handpicked by the shop co-owners and curators.

Tuan Vu Tran contributed stories, drawings, and games about his cats Lucky and Animal. Tuan's days are spent in-house in the marketing department working in graphic design and illustration, and his nights are spent passionately working on a series of interactive fiction gamebooks.

Raymond E. Mingst is an artist, writer, and curator (https:// RaymondEMingst.com). He has exhibited, curated, and collaborated with numerous galleries and institutions. He cofounded Curious Matter, a contemporary art gallery located in Jersey City, New Jersey (https://CuriousMatter. org). For occasional news and posts regarding his art practice and other diversions, Instagram is a place to find him (@RaymondEMingst).

Jay McQuirns spends his days watching dust bunnies intertwine with cat fur in the far reaches of his floor boards. He's also a cartoonist, and you can follow his exciting escapades on Instagram @JayMcQuirns.

Leah McNaughton Lederman, a Pushcart-nominated author, has created two volumes of *Café Macabre: A Collection of Horror Stories and Art by Women* (SourcePoint Press, 2019; 2021) and her own short story collection: *A Novel of Shorts: The Woman No One Sees* (2020). Her creative nonfiction has been published in the *River* and *South Review, Defenestration Mag,* and the *Wrath-Bearing Tree.* In 2022, Leah published *Beautifully Broken: The Katy Hayes Story,* about her cousin's life as a quadruple amputee. Currently, she is working on a memoir about growing up with a combat veteran father. Leah is active in several writing communities in the Midwest, where she lives with her husband and an assortment of children, cats, and dogs.

Melanie Rosato is a practicing artist who creates handbound books, zines, and collages. She has worked at museums, libraries, and universities where she has extensively researched and written for exhibits. She has also contributed reviews of literature and analysis of art historical subjects for blogs, as well as served as a community reviewer for the Feminist Library in London. She is from Scranton, Pennsylvania where she continues to live and work in the nonprofit industry.

Helen Kaucher (Hels) is an artist and maker in Pennsylvania. When she isn't working on products for her business, Hels' Bells Handmade, or experimenting with recycled art, she's probably outside, up in a tree moping, or surrounded by cats while she helps manage her family's tinned fish business. Find her on Instagram @OHelsBells or on her website: https://HelsBellsHandmade.com.

Erin Wu is a cake decorator, dancer, and ray of sunshine located in Athens, Georgia. She is a true cat lady and loves cats more than anything in this world. Her baby's name is Buster! Find her (and Buster) on Instagram: @E_WuHoo & @WuHoo_Cakes.

Caitlin Peck is an artist and illustrator in Philadelphia. Her delicate lines and surreal themes communicate the fragility, compulsion, and nuances of the relationships we carry with others, ourselves, and the universe we build around us. She has exhibited nationally and has appeared in publications online and in print internationally including *Witches Mag, Selcouth Journal, Venefica Magazine,* and *Feels Zine.* You can find her work on her website https://IAmCaitlinPeck.com.

Missy Kulik is an illustrator, cartoonist, zine maker, artist, and crafter. Originally from Pittsburgh, currently in Atlanta. Find her online at https://MissyKulik.com.

M.J. Fine lives in Philadelphia with her husband, Chris, and their twenty-year-old cat, Pippa. She has written about music, books, food, culture, and politics for a variety of publications, including *MAGNET*, *Philadelphia City Paper* (RIP), the *Courier-Post*, and the *Jewish Exponent*. M.J. and Chris think the optimal number of cats for their household is two, but Pippa thinks it is one, and she outranks them.

Jared Power loves his giant cat, Cooper, (a.k.a. Pooper, Pooper Scooper, Mr. Poop, or Dale). He also makes art of various sorts. Jared can be found at @EatBadArt on Instagram. You can reach him via DM or email JaredPowerArt@gmail.com, ask for Cooper pics, he will send them.

Marina Murayama is a soundscaper, educator, and electronic musician. Their collection of cat songs came from the album *Cat Dance Party* with the band the Snu Snu Dolls.

Originally from Onalaska, Wisconsin, **abby daleki** holds a BFA and MA in studio arts from Minnesota State University, Mankato and an MFA from the University of Delaware. They work primarily with acrylic paint. Currently, abby is an artist based out of Kansas City, Missouri and an Assistant Professor of art at Cottey College in Nevada, Missouri. They create bright-colored abstract object paintings that are hung on the wall, cut out from the frame, suspended from the ceiling, and/or pinned directly to the wall, exploring obsession and rumination, and using found and collected materials. Their work comments on male abstract painters and nods to female abstract artists like Lynda Benglis, Jessica Stockholder, and Judy Pfaff. In addition to painting, abby makes small, mixed-media drawings (usually during their 100 Day Project), adding in "junk-mail poetry." They will also draw your cat (if you'll let them), and, on occasion, they write short-read poems that sometimes stick you right where it hurts.

Vanessa Berry is a writer and artist and author of books including *Gentle and Fierce* and *Mirror Sydney*, and the zine series *I am a Camera*. She lives and works on unceded Gadigal land in Sydney, Australia. Her website is https://VanessaBerryWorld.wordpress.com and she is on Instagram @VanessaBerryWorld. The vintage postcard that accompanies "Haunted-House Cat" hangs above Vanessa's desk.

Yolie Contreras (she/her) is a Salvi–Chicanx zinester, writer and neurodivergent babe who has been creating zines for over ten years. Yolie specializes in perzines about sad-girl feelings, anxiety, depression, and OCD. She is based in Tucson, Arizona with her husband Billy and their two cats named Ricky and Fred. Find her on Instagram @Yolie4U.

Enx Eeden (he/they/neka) is a multidisciplinary artist and practitioner, author of *Two Spirit Traditions: Gender Animism* and *Turtle Island's Untold Intertribal Arts*. Originating from Lenapehoking, they were born in Philadelphia. His passions of ceremonial tattoo and poetry cultivated Sacred Canvas Collective, now a cosmos of diverse work. His compositions traverse music, visuals, humor, and healing to craft from a unified perspective. Finding inspiration from freeform art and queer resilience, Enx and their cat Akasha channel creation into magick. https://SacredCanvas.org

Ailbhe Pascal is a queer, disabled, storytelling witch who lives in occupied Coaquannock, Lenapehoking. Find Al writing poetry for their prayer tree, laughing at their own mistakes, or sharing moon meals with their chosen family. You can read their award-winning story "Canvas-Wax-Moon" (or listen to it as an audiobook) on Grist's Imagine 2200 website.

Alexis Campbell (she/her) lives in Phoenix with her human Greg, and their two cats, Midge and Roach. She owns a pet-sitting and dog-walking business, and spends her days reading about all the adventures local pets have with her employees and saving their photos to her phone . . . for business purposes, of course. When she's not running a business, she works on her dream of becoming a published YA author.

Courtney Stevenson is a printmaker with four cats, and the co-owner of Wider Awake Screen Printing.

Julia S. Owens was born in California, has lived in Orlando, Philadelphia, and Baltimore, and now resides in Tampa, Florida. She went to art school to learn how to draw and now sees herself as a community builder through art, writing, improv comedy, and playwork. Her collaborations include Mural Arts, Tree House Books, Smith Memorial Playground, and Rooted in Play.

Ed Kemp lives in beautiful Downtown Jersey City in an apartment he shares with the coolest of cool cats, a chatty gray, white, and black male tabby named Ashes. Rescued from the Jersey City incinerator, Ashes has been helping make zines for ten years now, and co-running The Word Distro since starting up back in 2014. Some of their work includes the zine series *Pencil of the Week* and *Touring America*.

Craig Wenner is a photographer. You can see more of his work on Instagram @CDWenn.

Ally Shwed is a cartoonist, writer, and editor from New Jersey. She received her MFA in Sequential Art from the Savannah College of Art & Design and has worked with the *Boston Globe*, the *Nib*, and First Second Books. Together with her partner Gerardo Alba, she runs Little Red Bird Press, a visual arts studio specializing in comics and printmaking. She currently calls Jersey City home, where she lives with Gerardo and their two cats, Egon and Schneider. https://AllyShwed.com

Ellen Muehlberger has basically one talent: playing with cats. She loves them, and she would rather play with—or sit quietly with, or blink at, or open a window for, or offer a lap to—cats than talk to people. When she's not playing with cats, she rides a bright orange bike and likes to go fast.

Kay Coster works in book publishing and lives in Denver, Colorado with Pete, Ernest, Sabrina, and Prunella (three of whom are cats).

Anna Lehr Mueser wrote an essay about a journey she took with her cat Mynah. Anna is a PhD student in the history and sociology of science, working on water, lost landscapes, and collective memory in the New York City watershed. She is also a book artist and letterpress printer.

True to her Gemini nature, **Jo-Jo Sherrow** draws comics, writes zines, and plays the piano. Her comics have previously been featured in the *Philadelphia City Paper*. Her work as an educator has spanned two decades and includes digital design, music, and yoga instruction. She lives with Brendan, a cute and irascible tabby cat. "Cat-Like" was previously published in the comic book, *Captcha #5*, from Pirouette Press in 2011.